GRADE 3

COMMON CORE
ENGLISH LANGUAGE ARTS
STATE STANDARDS

D1302325

Reviewers
Amy Corr • Douglas County School District • Highlands Ranch, CO
Tracie Baumgartner • Valley View School District • Bolingbrook, IL
Barbara Burns • Lammersville Unified School District • Mountain House, CA
Arlene Peters • Orange County Public Schools • Orlando, FL
Colleen Thomas • Sandwich Public Schools • Sandwich, MA
Holly Walker • Whitman-Hanson Regional School District • Hanson, MA

© 2012 **Perfection Learning**®
www.perfectionlearning.com

2 3 4 5 6 EB 16 15 14 13 12

EB/Ann Arbor, MI, USA
06/12

33137
ISBN-10: 0-7891-8224-6
ISBN-13: 978-0-7891-8224-1

Printed in the United States of America

To the Student

This book will help you review, practice, and master the English Language Arts Common Core State Standards. Here are the steps to follow to use this book.

1. Take the Tryout Test over Reading Literature, Reading Informational Text, and Language and check your answers. Use the chart at the bottom of this page to find out your strengths and weaknesses in the areas covered. Remember the questions that are hard for you to answer. They will be the types of questions you need to work on the most.

2. Work through the units that follow the Tryout Test. The lessons in each unit review example items and provide a practice test based on the standards. Fill in the Keeping Score chart on page 153 as you complete each practice test.

3. After completing all of the lessons, take the Mastery Test. Your score on this test will show your understanding of the Common Core State Standards.

4. Work through the Writing Test Workshops section of the book. These lessons will help you practice reading a writing prompt and taking different types of writing tests.

Reading Literature	Tryout Test Items	Mastery Test Items
Unit One—Key Ideas and Details		
Lesson 1 Ask and Answer Questions	7, 8	7, 13
Lesson 2 Central Ideas	9, 11, 13	2, 9, 19
Lesson 3 Characters and Plot	2, 10	1, 17, 18
Unit Two—Craft and Structure		
Lesson 4 Word Choice	6	3, 4, 14
Lesson 5 Structure and Point of View	3, 4	5, 8
Unit Three—Integration of Knowledge and Ideas		
Lesson 6 Illustrations	12	10
Lesson 7 Comparing and Contrasting Stories	14, 15, 16	11, 12, 13
Reading Informational Text	**Tryout Test Items**	**Mastery Test Items**
Unit Four—Key Ideas and Details		
Lesson 8 Ask and Answer Questions	18, 23	21, 29
Lesson 9 Main Ideas and Supporting Details	17, 19	20, 25
Unit Five—Craft and Structure		
Lesson 10 Text Structures and Point of View	27, 28, 29	26, 27, 28, 30
Lesson 11 Word Meanings	20, 22, 32	22, 31, 32
Unit Six—Integration of Knowledge and Ideas		
Lesson 12 Text Features and Illustrations	21, 30	23, 24
Lesson 13 Comparing and Contrasting Texts	24, 25, 26	34, 35
Language	**Tryout Test Items**	**Mastery Test Items**
Unit Seven—Nouns, Pronouns, and Verbs		
Lesson 14 Nouns	39, 44, 53	46, 50
Lesson 15 Pronouns	43, 45	40, 41
Lesson 16 Verbs	38, 42, 46	36, 37, 52
Unit Eight—Adjectives, Adverbs, and Conjunctions		
Lesson 17 Adjectives and Adverbs	41, 47	38, 49
Lesson 18 Conjunctions and Types of Sentences	33, 48, 49	39, 51, 52
Unit Nine—Capitalization, Punctuation, and Spelling		
Lesson 19 Capitalization	34, 50	48
Lesson 20 Punctuation	35, 36, 37	43, 45, 47
Lesson 21 Spelling	40, 51, 54	42, 44
Unit Ten—Vocabulary		
Lesson 22 Word Parts	1, 31	15, 16
Lesson 23 Word Use	5, 52	6, 33

Table of Contents

continued

Unit Nine—Capitalization, Punctuation, and Spelling

Unit Ten—Vocabulary

Writing

Standards Key: RL.3 = Reading Literature, Grade 3 Standard; RI.3 = Reading Informational Text, Grade 3 Standard; RL.3 = Language, Grade 3 Standard; W.3 = Writing, Grade 3 Standard.

Note: A complete correlation of Common Core State Standards can be found in the Grade 3 Teacher Guide.

Tryout Test: Part 1

Estimated time: 50 minutes

Directions: Read the passage. Then answer the questions that follow.

The River

1   As my aunt spread our blanket on the ground, I looked at the river. It flowed gently over smooth rocks and sparkled in the sun. I turned to see my two cousins scramble up to a small rocky ledge. Below them, the river formed an unusually deep pool. My cousins, Sam and Molly, called it their "swimming hole."

2   It was the first day of my visit to the North Woods with my cousins. I had never been to a place like this. Everywhere you looked, huge trees reached for the sky, and rivers wound their way through them. Back home, we have one wide river that slowly flows between two rows of tall buildings. Hundreds of cars cross it each day on concrete bridges. But here, Molly and Sam swam in rivers! They said I would love it.

3   Suddenly Sam hit the river like a cannonball, splashing water everywhere. Two seconds later his grinning face popped back up through the surface.

4   "Come on in, Kate!" he shouted. Then he swam to the shallow area near me. I was still watching him when I heard Molly's splash.

5   "Kate?" my uncle said. "Are you going to try it?"

6   I shrugged. I was thinking how I'd rather be at the YMCA pool back home. I loved it when my mom watched me do tricks there. Here, I wondered what might be <u>lurking</u> in this water. Some kind of biting fish? Plenty of nasty bugs had already made a feast of me.

7   For a long time I watched my cousins jump and swim. They never got tired of it. I also watched the other people near us. An entire family took turns jumping in as their large brown dog watched.

8   Finally, I decided to jump—just once. I was tired of watching. I climbed up the ledge and saw the cool water below. It looked miles away, but it invited me in. I took a deep breath and glanced to my right. Sitting near me was the dog, looking hot and bored.

9   I stepped off the ledge and kept my body straight. Feet first, I shot into the deep water. My body slowed down before it reached the bottom. Then I gave one big flap with my arms. Right before I reached the surface, I could hear and feel someone else plunge into the water.

10   The gentle current began to guide me down the river. As I swam I heard people on the shore shouting and laughing. My heart sank. Did I look that funny? Then I turned and saw the brown dog swimming behind me! I slowed down and let him catch up to me. When we reached the shallow water, I stood up and tried to run to the shore. I laughed as the dog splashed beside me.

11   "Kate!" my aunt shouted as we flew past her. "Please be <u>careful</u>!"

12   The dog beat me to the jumping ledge. He gave his soaked body a good shake. Everyone watched us. I jumped again, and sure enough, my new friend followed. Over and over we jumped and swam together until it was time to go.

13   "Great place!" I said to Molly while we folded the blanket. The dog barked from the ledge. Molly and Sam and I all waved good-bye.

14   Then Molly hugged me. "I'm glad you had fun," she said. "Can you come again next summer?"

1   Read this sentence from the passage.

"Please be careful!"

Knowing the meaning of the suffix *-ful* helps you understand that careful means—

A filled with care.

B less care.

C not able to care.

D care again.

2   At first, Kate does not want to go in the river because—

A she is afraid there might be biting fish in the water.

B she has never learned how to swim.

C the water is not as clean as it is in the pool at the YMCA.

D she doesn't know how to do any tricks.

3   The story is written from the point of view of—

A Kate

B the dog

C Molly

D Kate's aunt

4   Reread paragraph 6 that describes Kate's feelings about the river. Do you agree with Kate's point of view, or do you have a different opinion about the river? Write a few sentences describing your point of view. (3 points)

_____

_____

_____

_____

5   Read this sentence from paragraph 6 of the passage.

Here, I wondered what might be lurking in this water.

Which word has nearly the same meaning as lurking?

A floating

B prowling

C jumping

D swimming

GO ON

6 In paragraph 8, what does the narrator mean when she says the water "invited" her in?

   A The water actually spoke to her.

   B The water looked so good that she wanted to jump into it.

   C A person in the water invited her to jump.

   D Her aunt told her to jump in the water.

7 What did Kate first think when she heard people laughing?

   A Sam had jumped in after her.

   B The dog was following her.

   C The people thought she looked funny when she swam.

   D She had something stuck in her hair.

8 Describe how the narrator's feelings about the swimming hole change.
What causes the change? Use details from the story to support your answer. (3 points)

_____

_____

_____

_____

Directions: Read these two selections.

Cinderella

by Charles Perrault

1 In a far-off land, a lonely widower with a beautiful young daughter married a woman with two daughters. The man's daughter was sweet and kind, but the stepmother and her daughters were haughty and cruel. They were jealous of the girl's beauty. They treated her as a servant, making her sweep, scrub, and do laundry. She was even forced to remove ashes from the hearth, gaining her the name of Cinderella.

2 Then an invitation came to a palace <u>ball</u>. Stepmother and daughters were delighted and spent days selecting appropriate gowns. They acted as if Cinderella didn't exist.

3 At last the happy day came. The three women, dressed in finery, departed for the palace. After they left, Cinderella began weeping.

4 "Oh, I wish . . . I wish . . ." she sobbed.

5 Suddenly the room filled with light. Cinderella beheld an old woman holding a magic wand.

6 "Wh-who are you?" Cinderella asked.

7 "I am your fairy godmother," the woman said. "Tell me your wishes."

8   "I wish I could attend the ball," the girl answered. "But I have only rags to wear and no coach to deliver me."

9   The fairy godmother laughed kindly. "Nonsense," she said. "Run into the garden, and bring me a pumpkin."

10   Cinderella obeyed. The fairy godmother touched the pumpkin with her wand and turned it into a gleaming coach. Then she changed six mice into a team of horses and a rat into a regal coachman.

11   "How wonderful!" Cinderella exclaimed. "But my rags . . ."

12   With her wand, the godmother changed Cinderella's rags into a beautiful white gown. Then she gave her a pair of delicate glass slippers.

13   "You are ready for the ball," she said. "But be home by midnight. Or everything will turn back again."

14   Promising not to be late, Cinderella rode away joyfully. At the palace, the prince ran out to see who was arriving in such a splendid coach. He caught his breath when he beheld Cinderella. All the guests stopped dancing and stared. "Who is she?" people asked. "How beautiful she is!"

15   Cinderella danced with the prince all night. But just before midnight, she fled. The prince followed but could not overtake her. In her hurry, Cinderella dropped one of her glass slippers, which the prince found and carefully saved.

16   Just as Cinderella reached home, everything turned back to what it had been. Cinderella was left with one glass slipper. Feeling both sad and happy, she returned to her room.

17   The next day the prince swore to marry the woman whose foot the abandoned slipper fit. When his servant arrived at Cinderella's house, the two stepsisters tried in vain to fit into the tiny slipper.

18   Then Cinderella asked, "Might I try?"

19   Her sisters burst out laughing, but the servant agreed. To everyone's surprise, Cinderella's foot easily slid into the slipper. Smiling, Cinderella pulled out the other slipper and put it on too.

20   As the sisters watched in shock, the servant hurried Cinderella off to the palace. She married the prince and lived happily ever after.

Scarface

1   There once lived a great hunter who was invisible. Called Hidden One, he vowed to marry any woman who could see him.

2   Nearby lived two sisters. The older one was cruel and often tormented the younger one, burning her face with sticks. The younger sister, known as Scarface, was forced to go barefoot and wear rags. One day, the older sister bragged, "I'm going to marry Hidden One." She said to Scarface, "Of course, that's something you could never dream of."

3   Scarface remained silent.

4   When the older sister reached Hidden One's wigwam, his sister, Patient One, greeted her.

5   "Welcome," said Patient One. "My brother will return soon. Let us go meet him." She led the young woman to the lake.

6   "My brother comes," Patient One said, pointing along the shore. "Do you see him?"

7   "Yes," cried the young woman, though she saw no one.

8   The eyes of Patient One narrowed. "What is his shoulder strap?"

9   "A strip of rawhide," guessed the young woman.

10   Patient One frowned. "Let us go back."

11   They entered the wigwam, and a voice said, "Greetings, sister." The young woman looked around but saw no one. She watched as one moccasin, then another, appeared in mid-air and dropped to the floor. Then, bits of food rose from a tray and vanished. She asked Patient One, "Will I be married soon?"

12   Patient One answered angrily, "Do you think my brother would marry a liar and a fool?"

13   The young woman ran home crying. The next morning Scarface came to her.

14   "Sister, let me have skins to make moccasins and new clothes. It is my turn to visit Hidden One."

15   "You?" screamed the sister. "Why would he marry a pathetic thing like you?" Scarface had to wear an old pair of her father's moccasins and a dress made of tree bark.

16   She walked to Hidden One's wigwam. Patient One welcomed her and led her to the lake.

17   "My brother comes," Patient One said. "Do you see him?"

18   Scarface gazed along the shore. "Yes, I see him!"

19   "What is his shoulder strap?" Patient One asked.

20   "His strap is . . . the Rainbow!"

21   Patient One's eyes grew wide. "And his bowstring?"

22   "His bowstring is . . . the Milky Way!"

23   Patient One smiled. "Let us return."

24   At the wigwam, Patient One bathed Scarface with special water, making her scars disappear. Then Patient One brought out a beautiful wedding outfit. Scarface had just put it on when a voice said, "Greetings, sister."

25   "My brother," said Patient One, "you are discovered!"

26   Hidden One approached Scarface. "For years I have waited for a woman of pure heart and brave spirit. Only such a woman could see me. Now we will marry."

27   And so they did. Scarface received a new name, Lovely One. For she too had been hidden, but now was hidden no more.

Directions: Use "Cinderella" to answer the following questions.

9   The setting of the story is—

   A a kingdom in the mountains.

   B a small island.

   C a faraway country.

   D England in the 1800s.

---

10 Because Cinderella lost her slipper,—

   A the prince was able to find her.

   B the magic spell was broken.

   C Cinderella's stepsisters were mad.

   D the coach turned back into a pumpkin.

11 Study the flowchart of the plot of "Cinderella."

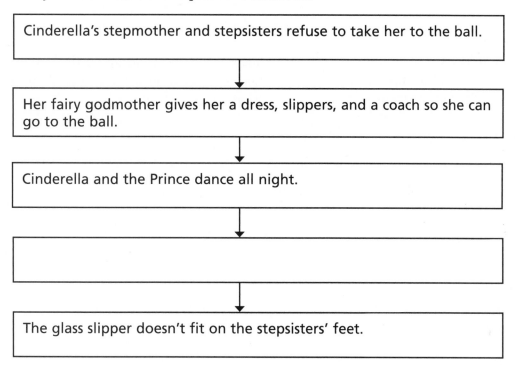

Cinderella's stepmother and stepsisters refuse to take her to the ball.

Her fairy godmother gives her a dress, slippers, and a coach so she can go to the ball.

Cinderella and the Prince dance all night.

The glass slipper doesn't fit on the stepsisters' feet.

Which sentence fits in the empty box?

   A The stepsisters acted as if Cinderella didn't exist.

   B The glass slipper fits on Cinderella's foot.

   C Cinderella and the Prince live happily ever after.

   D Just before midnight, Cinderella flees and drops a slipper.

Directions: Use "Scarface" to answer the following questions.

---

12 The illustration helps you understand which of the following details from the story?

   A Scarface had to wear a dress made of tree bark.

   B There once lived a great hunter who was invisible.

   C They entered the wigwam, and a voice said, "Greetings, sister."

   D Patient One bathed Scarface with special water, making her scars disappear.

GO ON

13 Read the following sentences.

Scarface received a new name, Lovely One. For she too had been hidden, but now was hidden no more.

What lesson or theme from the story do these sentences explain? Use details from the story to support your answer. (5 points)

_____

_____

_____

_____

_____

_____

_____

_____

Directions: Use both "Cinderella" and "Scarface" to answer the following questions.

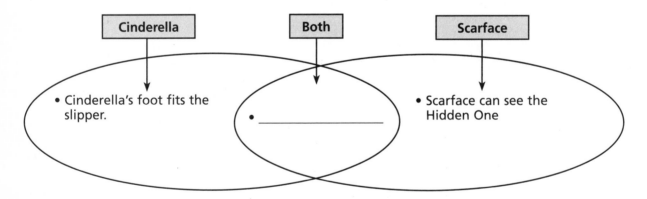

14 Which statement would fit under the **Scarface** section in the diagram?

A A fairy tale

B A myth

C A Native American folktale

D A fable

15 Which statement would fit under the **Both** section of the diagram?

   A Cinderella and Scarface are treated cruelly by their sisters.

   B Cinderella and Scarface have scars removed.

   C Cinderella and Scarface attend a ball.

   D Cinderella and Scarface receive new names.

16 A theme of both of the stories is—

   A Good people will be rewarded in the end.

   B Friendship is more important than riches.

   C Greediness will get you nowhere.

   D Beauty is only skin-deep.

Take a break. Then go on to Part 2.

Directions: Read the passage. Then answer the questions that follow.

Pass the Test!

1   How could dribbling a basketball have anything to do with schoolwork? Actually, when our bodies are active, our brains become active as well. People who study kids have made some interesting discoveries. They have found that when kids exercise, their brains work better. It's true! Physical activity helps blood flow to our brain. It also helps cell growth.

2   Did you know that students who exercise every day do better on tests? When a student's body is active, the brain makes decisions more quickly and remembers better. Kids who are physically active enjoy <u>school</u> more and tend to like themselves more. The physical activity allows them to relax.

3   All that comes from being physically active? Yes, and there is more. Researchers studied kids who are physically active and those who are not. They discovered that active kids are less likely to get in trouble at school. They also found out that active kids are more likely to have other healthy habits. They eat more fruits and vegetables. They watch less television. They wear their seat belts. They are even less likely to smoke when they get older. Wow!

4   To stay healthy, experts say kids should exercise at least 60 minutes every day. Every physical activity counts—walking, riding a bike, playing basketball, swimming. There are too many physical activities to count! So just choose a few and get busy. Your body *and* your brain will be glad you did.

www.photos.com

17 What is the main idea of the passage?

   A When kids exercise, their brains work better.

   B Physical activity helps cell growth.

   C People who study kids have made interesting discoveries.

   D Riding a bike is an example of physical activity.

18 Which question does paragraph 2 answer?

   A What does basketball have to do with schoolwork?

   B How much should a kid exercise each day?

   C How does physical activity make the brain work better?

   D Is watching television a healthy habit?

19 This web shows details about children who are physically active.

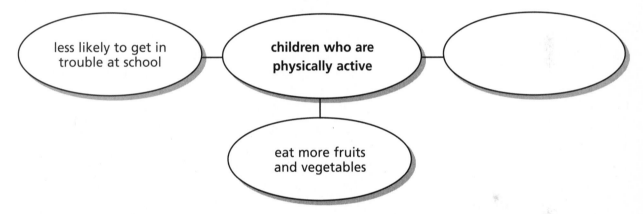

Which BEST completes the web?

   A more likely to watch television

   B less likely to smoke when older

   C less likely to wear seat belt

   D less likely to enjoy school

20 Read this dictionary entry for the word <u>school</u>.

> **school (skool) 1.** *n.* Place for teaching children. **2.** *n.* College. **3.** *v.* To teach or train someone. **4.** *n.* Large group of the same type of fish.

Which meaning of the word <u>school</u> is used in paragraph 2?

   A definition 1

   B definition 2

   C definition 3

   D definition 4

21 Read the book's table of contents.

Which chapter begins on page 10?

A "How We Used to Live"

B "How We Live Today"

C "Why Run?"

D "Pass the Test!"

22 Based upon the context of the passage, explain the meaning of the word *physical*. Then use *physical* in a new sentence. (3 points)

_____

_____

_____

_____

Directions: Read both passages. Then answer the questions that follow.

Chapter One

The Complete Book of Birds

The monk parakeet, a popular pet in the United States, comes originally from South America. It is the only kind of parrot that does not nest in a cavity, or hole. Instead, monk parakeets build a structure of sticks. It can hold one nest or many that have individual rooms or chambers. The birds usually construct these outdoor houses—or repair their old ones—in the spring. They live in them year-round. Some of the nests are enormous and may weigh over 2000 pounds!

THE DAILY NEWS

Monk Parakeets Set Up House

By Cody Johnson
DAILY STAFF WRITER

In a neighborhood on the south side of Chicago lives a colony of monk parakeets. These birds have lived in the area since about 1980, when about a dozen of them probably escaped from their owner. Now the colony has expanded to 250 birds and has 40 nests. Monk parakeets are the only parakeets that live in groups rather than individual nests.

How do the birds survive in the frigid winters in Chicago? They cluster in their nests. Citizens in the area make sure the birds are fed. In the summer they feed on grasses and fruit growing on trees.

23 Which passage gives the best information about how monk parakeets survive outdoors in the winter? Use information from the article to support your answer. (3 points)

_____

_____

_____

_____

_____

_____

_____

_____

_____

_____

_____

24 Both articles are mainly about—

   A a nest in Chicago.

   B monk parakeets.

   C what parakeets eat.

   D what nests are made of.

25 "Monk Parakeets Set Up House" gives more information about—

   A a colony of monk parakeets in Chicago.

   B where monk parakeets come from.

   C why the birds make good pets.

   D when the birds make their nests.

26 "The Complete Book of Birds" gives more information about—

   A what color monk parakeets are.

   B when some pet birds escaped.

   C why citizens feed the birds.

   D the size and weight of nests.

Directions: Read the passage. Then answer the questions that follow.

Johnny Appleseed

Close your eyes. Picture rows and rows of apple trees. That's what John Chapman did. However, he didn't just picture the trees. He set out to make this idea come true. Chapman spent almost 50 years planting apple trees in the American wilderness. Because of his work, he was called Johnny Appleseed.

In the early 1800s, many people were moving westward. By law, each family had to plant 50 apple trees on their new land. The idea was to make sure they would have food.

Chapman saw a way to help the settlers. He was good at growing plants. He decided to go ahead of the settlers. He planned to plant apple trees.

Chapman was careful about where he planted these trees. He was careful about how he planted them too. He didn't just scatter seeds wherever he went. He spent forever looking for a place with good soil. When he found the right spot, he cleared the land. When the soil was ready, he planted the seeds. Before he left, he built a fence to protect the trees.

When people arrived, they didn't have to plant a single apple tree. Chapman had done all the work for them! Soon stories about him began to spread. One story told about how he saved a wolf from a trap. The wolf became his friend. It traveled with him for a while.

In his travels, Chapman worked alone. His life was simple. He walked barefoot through the wilderness. All he carried was a bag of apple seeds and his camping gear. He lived in simple shelters. Sometimes he made a hut out of tree bark. Other times he slept on a bed of leaves or on the ground near a small fire.

Chapman mostly lived alone. Even so, he had many friends. Aside from the settlers, he made friends with many Native American tribes. He learned their languages and their customs. They grew to trust him. Sometimes they even let him join their meetings. When a conflict happened between settlers and Native Americans, Chapman often was able to help.

As he traveled from place to place, Chapman sold apple seeds and trees to many people. He let them pay in different ways. Some paid with money. Others paid with used clothes or food or with the promise to pay later. What was most important to Chapman was that they planted the trees.

During his lifetime, he planted apple trees in Pennsylvania, Ohio, Kentucky, Illinois, and Indiana. Today, many of his apple trees still bear fruit! John Chapman is truly an American hero.

27 Read the chart below. It shows the steps John Chapman followed to plant an apple orchard.

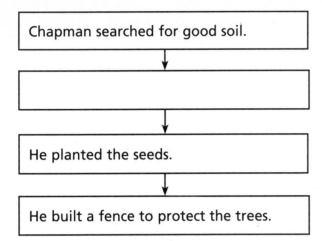

Chapman searched for good soil.

↓

He planted the seeds.

↓

He built a fence to protect the trees.

Which of these belongs in the empty box?

A He built a shelter.

B He collected money.

C He scattered the seeds.

D He cleared the land.

28 What happened as a result of Chapman learning the languages and customs of the Native Americans?

A The Native Americans helped him plant apple trees.

B The Native Americans left the settlers alone.

C Chapman went to live with a Native American tribe.

D Chapman was able to help solve conflicts between Native Americans and the settlers.

29 Which of the following sentences from the text BEST describes the author's point of view about Chapman?

A *Chapman spent almost 50 years planting apple trees in the American wilderness.*

B *He was good at growing plants.*

C *One story told about how he saved a wolf from a trap.*

D *John Chapman is truly an American hero.*

Directions: Look at this page from an informational book on Redwood National Park. Answer the questions that follow.

Redwood Forest

www.photos.com

Ferns

The most common ferns in the redwood forests are the bracken fern, lady fern, western sword fern, and five-fingered fern. Driving and walking the paths of the redwoods, visitors will spot many of these plants.

Five-fingered ferns were important to the Yuroks. The black stems were stripped off and used to make patterns on baskets.

All ferns depend on water to reproduce. The plants produce very small seeds called *spores*. These spores blow easily from one location to the next. Once they land in water, they begin to sprout.

Giant Horsetails

Giant horsetails live among the ferns. These plants have been around for millions of years. Giant horsetails have groups of pointy leaves growing on tall stems. These plants like to grow in wet areas and need water to reproduce.

Plants You Can Eat

The redwood parks are home to several plants that are safe for humans to eat. However, visitors should never eat a plant unless they are sure it is edible.

Raspberry, thimbleberry, salmonberry, and blackberry bushes all grow alongside the roads. These berries need a lot of sunlight to thrive.

Black and red huckleberry plants are found deep within the forest. These berries need a drier environment and less sunlight.

Wild strawberries grow on the grasslands near Bald Hills Road. One plant used by the American Indians was the hazelnut tree. The Indians ate the nuts and used the wood to make baskets.

Wild Strawberry

www.photos.com

32

GO ON

30   What is the purpose of the captions in the pictures?

   A to tell about plants

   B to describe the photos

   C to tell about giant horsetails

   D to describe edible plants

31   Study the following sentence.

   These plants like to grow in wet areas and need water to <u>reproduce</u>.

   The prefix *re-* in the word <u>produce</u> means—

   A against.

   B above.

   C again.

   D stop.

32   Study the following sentence.

   The Redwood parks are home to several plants that are safe for humans to eat. However, visitors should never eat a plant unless they are sure it is <u>edible</u>.

   Based upon the context, the word <u>edible</u> means—

   A not safe to eat.

   B not safe to drink.

   C safe to eat.

   D a dangerous plant.

> **Take a break. Then go on to Part 3.**

Directions: Read each question and choose the best answer.

33 Which of the following is a simple sentence?

   A Mom loves orange juice.

   B Mom loves orange juice, but my brother likes apple juice better.

   C Even though my mom loves orange juice, she doesn't drink it every day.

   D Mom loves orange juice, and my brother loves apple juice.

34 Which sentence uses capitalization correctly?

   A My Teacher's name is Mr. Jon tibbets.

   B My teacher's name is mr. Jon Tibbets.

   C My teacher's name is Mr. Jon Tibbets.

   D My Teacher's name is Mr. Jon Tibbets.

35 Which sentence uses commas correctly?

   A Karen loves to read books, watch movies, and play tennis.

   B Karen, loves to read books, watch movies and play tennis.

   C Karen loves to read books watch movies and play tennis.

   D Karen loves to read books watch movies, and play tennis.

36 Which of the following sentences is correct?

   A Cammie borrowed her mothers shoes.

   B Cammie borrowed her mother's shoes.

   C Cammie borrowed her mothers's shoes.

   D Cammie borrowed her mother"s shoes.

37 Which sentence uses punctuation correctly?

   A Mother asked "Did Dad call?"

   B Mother asked, "Did Dad call?"

   C "Mother asked, Did Dad call?"

   D Mother asked Did Dad call?

38 Which verb BEST completes the sentence?

Grandma Lally _____ in Texas.

   A live

   B living

   C be living

   D lives

39 What is the noun in this sentence?

Tyler loves to run.

A Tyler

B loves

C to

D run

40 In which sentence is the underlined word spelled correctly?

A Our team <u>finaly</u> won the game.

B In the bleachers, the parents <u>cheered</u>.

C We <u>shooke</u> hands with the other team.

D Everyone <u>playd</u> their best.

41 What is the adjective in the sentence?

Paul's younger brother is in kindergarten.

A Paul's

B younger

C brother

D kindergarten

42 Which verb BEST completes the sentence?

Last week Harold _____ to the new space museum.

A will go

B goes

C went

D goed

43 Choose the correct pronoun.

Jackie and Ming lost _____ homework folders on the bus.

A his

B him

C her

D their

44 Which of the following plural nouns is correct?

A boxs

B mans

C women

D tooths

45 Which part of speech takes the place of a noun?

   A verb

   B adjective

   C adverb

   D pronoun

46 Which of the following parts of speech shows action or being?

   A nouns

   B pronouns

   C adverbs

   D verbs

47 Choose the correct adjective form for the following sentence.

   Of all the students in the class, Michael's time for the mile run was _____.

   A fastest

   B more faster

   C faster

   D more fastest

48 Use a conjunction to create a compound sentence from the two simple sentences below. Be sure to use correct punctuation. (2 points)

   My mom took us to the store to buy groceries. My dad stayed home and watched the baby.

   _____

   _____

49 Which of the following sentences contains standard English?

   A I ain't going to write about my summer vacation.

   B She be going to buy a new bike when she gets the money.

   C I want to save my money for a new skateboard.

   D The skateboard he was riding was way rad.

50 Which of the following sentences contains correct capitalization?

   A I want to see a Movie at the Mall.

   B The movie is called *Point of No Return*.

   C It stars my favorite Actor, Gerome Smith.

   D The movie was filmed in hollywood, california.

GO ON

51 Which of the following underlined words is spelled correctly?

   A My <u>naybor's</u> house is black and white.

   B They have a basketball hoop in <u>thier</u> driveway.

   C Their house is <u>beutiful</u>.

   D I like playing at their house <u>a lot</u>.

52 Which of the following means nearly the same thing as the word <u>know</u> in this sentence?

I <u>know</u> that answer is correct.

   A think

   B believe

   C wonder if

   D am sure

53 Which of the following is an abstract noun?

   A love

   B puppy

   C queen

   D school

54 Which of the following underlined words is correct?

   A We <u>walkked</u> home from school.

   B We <u>stopped</u> at the gas station to get some water.

   C We <u>jumpped</u> on my trampoline.

   D I enjoy <u>runing</u> on the path near my house.

Points Earned/Total = _____/67

Reading Literature Lesson 1

Ask and Answer Questions

Review the Standard (RL.3.1)

- Ask and answer questions about a text
- Refer to the text as a basis for answers

Q: How can asking questions help me understand **literature**?

A: Stories, poems, and plays are **literature**, or **fiction.** The following chart will help you understand questions to ask before, during, and after reading.

Before Reading (Make predictions)	During Reading (Make predictions and understand the story)	After Reading (Understand the story, make connections)
• Based upon the title and pictures, what do I think the story is about? • What do I think will happen in the story?	• Who are the characters? • What is happening in the story? • Why did the character do or say what he/she did? • What do I think will happen next? • What does _____ mean? • What do I think of when I read _____?	• What did I like or not like about the story? • How did the story make me feel? • What was the main idea of the story? • Have I experienced something similar to the events in the story?

Q: How should I answer questions about the text?

A: Any answers about the text must be based upon what the text says. Go back and look at the text, underlining main ideas and details. Include these details in your answer. Even opinions about the text (which aren't right or wrong) must be based upon things clearly stated in the story.

GO ON

Directions: Read the following passage. Then answer the questions that follow.

Curtis's Pet Problem

1   As Curtis walked out of the pet store, he held a tiny black kitten in his arms. "I think I'll call her Eve," Curtis said to his mother, "because she's dark like the evening sky."

2   When Curtis got home, he set out bowls of food and water for Eve. The kitten tasted the food and began to purr loudly. Curtis petted Eve gently. "We're going to be good friends," he said.

3   Curtis had always wanted a cat. Many of his friends had dogs for pets. Curtis agreed that dogs are often friendlier than cats. They can also do useful things, such as guard the owner's home. But Curtis thought dogs needed too much attention. Dogs have to be taken for walks several times a day. Cats, on the other hand, take care of themselves. They are quieter and cleaner than dogs. Curtis also liked the way they curled up on laps. Curtis went to sleep that night feeling happy that he finally had a cat of his own.

4   The next morning, Curtis woke up to find his new kitten sleeping next to his pillow. He reached over to pet Eve's soft fur. Suddenly he started to sneeze. His eyes began to water too. As Curtis got dressed, he noticed a red rash on his skin.

5   Curtis's mother took him to see Dr. Ledo right away. Dr. Ledo examined Curtis carefully. Then she said, "Your mother tells me that you have a new kitten. Some people become sick when they are around cats. I'm afraid that you are one of those people. If you keep your kitten, you will start to feel even worse."

1 Which is the BEST question to ask after reading the title and the first paragraph of the passage?

    A How will Curtis's new pet become a problem?

    B Will Curtis buy a dog?

    C Where does Curtis live?

    D Where did Curtis buy his new kitten?

2 Which is the BEST question to ask after reading paragraph 4?

    A Why did the kitten sleep next to Curtis?

    B Does the kitten have a bed to sleep in?

    C Why is Curtis sneezing and having other reactions?

    D Where is Curtis's bedroom?

3 What do you think Curtis will do next? Support your prediction with details from the passage. (5 points)

_____

_____

_____

_____

Example 1 asks you to think about questions you should ask before reading the passage. The best type of question is one that helps you make a prediction, or an educated guess, about the passage. The title reveals that Curtis has a pet who is a problem. The first paragraph reveals that Curtis has just purchased a new cat. The best question to ask is **choice A**, *How will Curtis's new pet become a problem?*

Example 2 asks you to think about the type of questions you should ask while reading a passage. Paragraph 4 describes Curtis's sneezing, watering eyes, and rash. The best question to ask is, *Why is Curtis sneezing and having other reactions?,* or **choice C**.

Example 3 asks you to make a prediction about what will happen after the story ends. Although the answer to this question will not be found directly in the text, your prediction should be based upon what you do know. You know that Curtis is allergic to his new kitten. You also know that Curtis wanted a cat instead of a dog because they are more independent, quieter, and cleaner than dogs. A good answer will contain details from the passage to support your prediction.

Good: *Because the doctor says that he will become sicker if he keeps his cat, I predict that Curtis will give up his cat. Curtis likes cats because they are clean, quiet, and can curl up on laps. I think Curtis will try to find a small dog that doesn't shed and can sit on his lap.*

Poor: *Curtis will have to get rid of his cat.*

Directions: Read the following poem. Then answer the questions that follow.

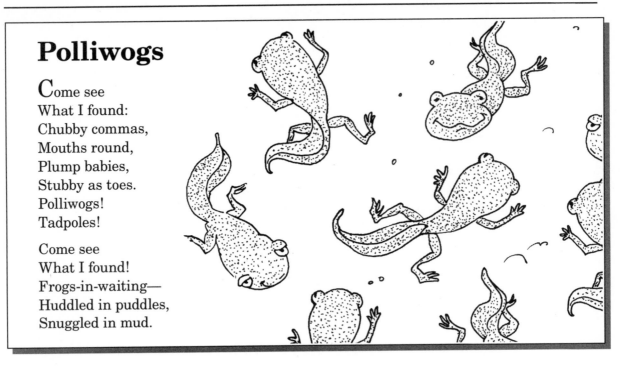

Polliwogs

Come see
What I found:
Chubby commas,
Mouths round,
Plump babies,
Stubby as toes.
Polliwogs!
Tadpoles!

Come see
What I found!
Frogs-in-waiting—
Huddled in puddles,
Snuggled in mud.

4   What would be the BEST question to ask while reading this poem?

   A How deep is a puddle?

   B How is a comma used in a sentence?

   C Why do frogs hop?

   D What is a polliwog?

5   Which of the following is a good question to ask after reading the last five lines of the poem?

   A To whom is the writer talking?

   B Do polliwogs become frogs?

   C Why do polliwogs like mud?

   D Does the poem take place after a rainstorm?

6   What descriptive words from the poem help you understand what polliwogs look like? Use examples from the poem to support your answer. (3 points)

_____

_____

_____

_____

_____

Central Ideas

Review the Standard (RL.3.2)

- **Recount fables, folktales,** and **myths** from diverse cultures
- Find a central message, lesson, or moral of a text

Q: How do I **recount fables, folktales,** and **myths**?

A: *Recount* means to retell. Another word that means "recount" is *summarize.* When you tell your mom about the basketball game you played at recess, you are retelling the story of the game. You describe the events of the game in the order in which they happened, or chronological order. You probably use words like *first, then, next, after,* and *later* to explain what happened. You recount a story in the same way that you retell your basketball story, by explaining the main events in the story in chronological order.

Q: What are **fables, folktales,** and **myths**?

A: This chart will help you understand the difference between **fables, folktales,** and **myths**.

Type of Story	Characteristics of the Plot
Fable	A fable teaches a useful lesson and often has animals in it who speak and act like humans.
Folktale	A folktale is a traditional story with a moral or lesson handed down by people of a region from one generation to another.
Myth	A myth is an old story that has been handed down through time that tells about gods and heroes or explains events in nature.

Q: How do I determine the **central message, lesson,** or **moral** in a fable, folktale, or myth?

A: To find the **central message** or **lesson,** ask: *What does the main character learn from the events in the story?* Some fables will contain a sentence at the end of the story stating the lesson that the main character learned. This is called the *moral.*

GO ON

Directions: Read the following passage. Then answer the questions that follow.

The Golden Touch

Long ago there lived a certain king named King Midas. Bacchus, the merry god of the vine, told King Midas that he had been so kind to him that he would grant him a wish.

King Midas couldn't believe his ears. "I can wish for anything? Then I want to have a golden touch so that everything I touch will turn to gold."

"But King Midas, you already have all the gold you need," declared Bacchus. "Isn't there something else you would wish for?"

Bacchus could not change King Midas's mind, so he granted the wish and then waved good-bye. Just as he was leaving, King Midas's hand brushed a twig and it instantly turned to gold. King Midas couldn't believe his good fortune!

King Midas ran around the courtyard touching everything he could and watching it turn to gold. He shouted with joy, and his servants all rushed out to observe this unusual behavior.

King Midas finally tired of this work and ordered that his supper be brought before him. He was starving from all of the activities. But every bite he tried to eat turned to gold, so he was unable to eat. He soon realized he would starve if this continued.

"Please come back, Bacchus! I am so sorry I made this wish. I have learned my lesson."

Bacchus returned and said, "You were greedy and foolish, my friend, but I will forgive you. Go to the river and wash, and the magic touch will be gone."

It happened just like Bacchus had said. King Midas returned home and happily ate his supper.

1   This story is—

   A a fable.

   B a folktale.

   C a myth.

   D none of the above.

2 Recount the events in the passage in a short paragraph. Be sure to include only the main events of the story. (5 points)

_____

_____

_____

_____

_____

_____

_____

_____

_____

_____

3 What is the central lesson of the story?

A Don't trust the gods.

B The gods know best.

C It is better to forgive than to hold a grudge.

D Don't be greedy; you may not like what you get.

For **Example 1**, you must decide what type of story "The Golden Touch" is. Consider the details of the story. The characters are a king and a god. The god has magical powers to grant wishes. These clues point to **choice C** as the correct answer.

Example 2 asks you to **recount**, or retell, the passage. Your retelling should include only the major events of the story. These events should be explained in chronological order, or the order in which they occur.

Good: *The god Bacchus granted King Midas one wish. King Midas wished for a golden touch so that everything he touched would turn to gold. King Midas ran around touching everything. When he was hungry, he touched his food and it turned to gold. King Midas realized that he would starve to death, so he asked Bacchus to take back his wish. Bacchus told Midas that he had been too greedy in his wish.*

Poor: *King Midas was greedy and asked Bacchus for a golden touch. His servants ran out to see him turning everything to gold. Bacchus told him to go wash in the river and the magic touch would be gone.*

Example 3 asks you to identify the **lesson** of the story. Go back to the story and review the events. Think about what the main character learns. Bacchus tells King Midas that he was greedy and foolish to wish for the golden touch. King Midas realizes that having money isn't the most important thing in the world. The answer choice that best fits this is, *Don't be greedy; you may not like what you get,* or **choice D**.

Directions: Read the following passage, and then answer the questions that follow.

This story was first told in Africa long ago. Africans brought the story here when they came to America. They continued to tell it to their children and grandchildren in this country.

The Knee-High Man

There was once a Knee-High Man who lived by the swamp. More than anything he wanted to be big, so he decided that he was going to ask advice from the biggest thing he knew. So he went to see Mr. Horse.

"Mr. Horse, how can I get big?"

"Well, you eat a lot of corn and then you run around and around and then you will be as big as I am," replied the horse.

The Knee-High Man tried to do what Mr. Horse had said, but his belly hurt and his legs hurt and he didn't get any bigger. Next he decided to go ask Brer Bull for advice.

"Well, you eat a lot of grass and then you shout in a deep voice and you will be as big as I am," replied Brer Bull.

The Knee-High Man did what Brer Bull said, but his belly hurt from the grass and his neck hurt from shouting and he didn't get any bigger.

"I think I need to ask Mr. Hoot Owl. He is smart and he will know the answer," said the Knee-High Man.

After hearing the question, Mr. Hoot Owl said, "Anybody ever pick a fight with you?"

"No," replied the Knee-High Man.

"Then you don't need to be any bigger," suggested Mr. Hoot Owl.

"But I want to be tall to see far away."

"Can't you climb a tree and see far away?"

"Well, yeah, I guess," replied the Knee-High Man.

"Well," declared Mr. Hoot Owl, "I don't think you need to be any bigger in body, but you sure need to be bigger in brain!"

4 Retell the events of the passage in one paragraph. (3 points)

_____

_____

_____

_____

_____

_____

5 This story is most likely a folktale because—

A it has gods and heroes.

B it has been told and retold by people from Africa.

C it explains how the old became wise.

D it doesn't teach a lesson.

6 Why does the Knee-High Man go to the horse, the bull, and the owl?

A He wants to be big.

B He wants to be a horse.

C He wants to become wise.

D He wants to learn to fly.

7 What is the central message of this story?

A Bigger is better.

B Be happy with who you are.

C Grass helps people get taller.

D Short people need bigger brains.

GO ON

Reading Literature Lesson 3

Characters and Plot

Review the Standard (RL.3.3)

- Describe a **character's traits**, **motivations**, and **feelings**
- Explain how a character's actions contribute to the **plot**

Q: What are a **character's traits**, **motivations**, and **feelings**?

A: The following chart explains the terms *character traits*, *motivations*, and *feelings*.

	Answers the question(s)	**Examples**
Character Traits	What is the character like? How would you describe the character?	Fearful, Shy, Proud
Motivations	Why did the character do that?	He was afraid, so he . . . Because he was angry, he . . .
Feelings	How does the character feel?	She feels afraid. She feels tired.

Q: How do I figure out a **character's traits**, **motivations**, and **feelings**?

A: Sometimes the story will clearly describe how a character feels: *Sally felt sad and lonely.* Other times you will have to look at what the character says and does and then draw your own conclusion. Consider this example:

Sally went into her new room in her new house and closed the door. She threw herself on her bed and began to cry.

By her actions, you can guess, or infer, that Sally is sad and lonely.

Q: How do a character's actions contribute to the **plot** in a story?

A: The **series of events** in a story is called *plot*. Sometimes it is helpful to use a flowchart to help you think about how a character's actions influence the events in the story.

Event 1

↓

Event 2

↓

Event 3

↓

Event 4

Directions: Read the following passage. Then answer the questions that follow.

The Pied Piper of Hamelin

1 Long ago, the town of Hamelin had a problem. Rats. The rodents swarmed into town searching for food, water, and warm places to sleep. The townsfolk were desperate to get rid of these pests.

2 One day, a stranger came to town and made an offer. He said he would rid the town of every single rat. His fee for this service was one schilling per rat.

3 In desperation, the town agreed. "Please start immediately," they begged.

4 The stranger took out a pipe, and he began to play a beautiful tune. From nooks and crannies, the rats began to come. They followed the piper as he walked through the streets of town. As he played the delightful music, they followed him out of town and to the river. There, the piper stood on the banks of the river. One by one, every rat jumped in the water, drowned, and was swept away.

5 When the piper returned to town for his payment, the townsfolk grew angry. "How dare you ask us to pay!" they cried. "Any decent human being would help others at no cost." And they went into their houses and slammed their doors.

6 Without another word, the piper left town.

7 On Sunday, the townsfolk went to church as usual. The children played outside. As they played, they noticed a stranger dressed in brightly colored clothing. He was playing a delightful tune on his pipe. Laughing and skipping, the children followed the piper.

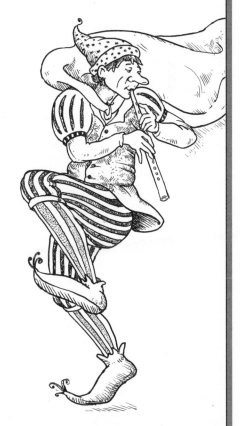

8 The piper led the children to the hills outside of town. There, he stood beside the mouth of a large cave. One by one, every child danced into the cave. When the last one had entered, the piper stopped his music. Like magic, a huge rock appeared, sealing up the cave. The piper turned and walked away, never to be seen again.

9 But all the children were not in the cave. One child who had sprained her ankle remained outside. She had not been able to keep up with the rest. And even though she told everyone in town where the children were, no one could get them back.

10 The piper had taught everyone a harsh lesson. It is best to pay the piper or worse things will happen.

 GO ON

1   In paragraphs 1–3, the townspeople could be described as—

   A kind.

   B welcoming.

   C angry.

   D desperate.

2   The chart shows the order of events in the story.

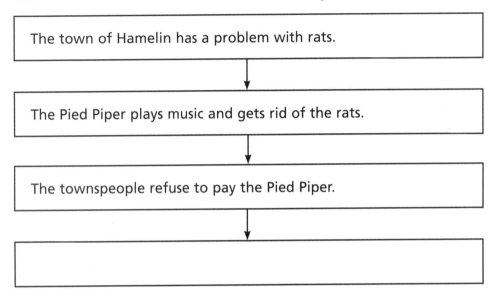

Which statement belongs in the empty box?

   A The Pied Piper plays music and leads the children of Hamelin into a cave, where
       they are trapped.

   B The children are released from the cave.

   C A stranger comes to Hamelin and offers to get rid of the rats.

   D The Pied Piper plays music and leads the children into the river, where they are
       drowned.

3   Because one of the children can't keep up with the others,—

   A she is never seen again.

   B she tells the townspeople where the children are.

   C the townspeople are able to rescue the children.

   D the townspeople catch the Pied Piper.

   Example 1 asks you to think about a **character trait** of the townspeople. A close look
at paragraphs 1–3 reveals that they have a problem with rats, and they are desperate to
get rid of them. **Choice D** is the best answer.
   For **Example 2,** you must think about the **plot** of the story and how a character's
actions influence the events in the story. Think about what happens because the
townspeople refuse to pay the piper. You know that this action results in the Pied Piper
taking all the children in the town and luring them into a cave. The correct answer is
choice A.

Example 3 also asks you to think about how a **character's actions** affect the plot of the story. Reread paragraph 9. Because one child had sprained her ankle and couldn't keep up with the others, she is not caught in the cave. *She tells the townspeople where the children are*, or **choice B**, is the correct answer.

◎ Try It On Your Own

4   Because the townspeople refuse to pay the Pied Piper, we can conclude that they are—

   A unthankful.

   B revengeful.

   C poor.

   D happy.

5   Based upon the Pied Piper's actions at the end of the story, we can conclude that he is—

   A kind.

   B revengeful.

   C rich.

   D proud.

6   Explain how the townspeople's choice not to pay the Pied Piper influences the events in the story. (3 points)

_____

_____

_____

_____

_____

_____

Test-Taking Tips

1 Always read the whole selection carefully. Look for clues to help you understand the characters. You can understand what characters are like from their words and actions. You can understand a character's motivation by asking yourself, *Why did he/she do that?*

2 To answer a question about the plot, ask yourself, *What is the main problem in the story?* and *How is the problem solved?* Think about how the character's actions cause things to happen in the story.

3 To find the theme, think about the lesson the author wants the reader to learn. Sometimes a lesson or moral is stated at the end of a fable or folktale.

Go for it!

Unit One Practice Test

Directions: Read the passage. Then answer the questions that follow.

The Magic Fish

Once upon a time there was a poor fisherman who lived with his wife in a hut by the sea. Every day he went fishing and every day he brought home fish to eat. One day he felt a mighty tug on his line. He pulled and pulled, and finally up came a huge fish!

"Quick, put me back into the water. I am really a magic fish."

"Well, if you are really magic, I will throw you back," replied the fisherman.

The fisherman's wife was angry that her husband had thrown the fish back. She ordered her husband to go ask the fish for a nice house if it was truly magic.

The fisherman did what his wife said, and when he returned home, there was a nice house where his old house had been.

Because the wife was greedy, she didn't stay happy for very long. Soon she wanted to live in a castle, so she sent her husband back to talk to the magic fish. When he returned home again, there stood a castle where the nice house had been.

Again, because she was greedy, she didn't stay happy for long and wanted to be queen of the land. Once again, her husband asked the magic fish and it happened. Of course, that didn't keep her happy for long because she wanted to be queen of the sun and moon as well.

When the fisherman asked the magic fish, he replied, "Your wife is too greedy. Return home and you will find the house you started with." The fisherman went home and there stood his old house with his wife inside. That is the house he has to this day.

1 Which detail from the story shows that the fisherman is hardworking?

   A He is poor.

   B He lives by the sea.

   C He goes fishing every day.

   D He catches a magic fish.

2 Which of the following is a good question to ask to help you understand what motivates the wife?

   A Why does she order her husband to ask the fish for a nice house?

   B Who is the wife?

   C Where does the wife live?

   D Why does the husband obey his wife's demand to ask for a nice house?

3 Which detail from the story shows that the wife is greedy?

  A She is not satisfied with what she has.

  B She lives in a hut.

  C She eats fish every day.

  D She is bossy to her husband.

4 All of the following details should be included in a retelling of the plot EXCEPT—

  A One day the fisherman felt a tug on his line.

  B At first the fisherman threw the magic fish back into the water.

  C The wife was not satisfied with a nice house and sent her husband back to ask the magic fish for a castle.

  D The fisherman went home to find his old house and his wife inside.

5 How does the fisherman's refusal to stand up to his wife contribute to the plot of the story?

  A He wants to become king of the sun and moon.

  B He keeps going back to the magic fish to ask for more wishes.

  C He continues to catch bigger and better fish.

  D He becomes a better fisherman.

6 What is the lesson, or moral, of the story? Support your answer using details from the text. (3 points)

_____

_____

_____

_____

_____

Points Earned/Total = _____ /8

Reading Literature Lesson 4

Word Choice

Review the Standards (RL.3.4, L.3.4.a, L.3.5.a)

- Explain **literal** and **nonliteral** meanings based upon the **context** of the words

Q: What is the difference between **literal** and **nonliteral** meanings of words?

A: The **literal** meanings of words are the dictionary definitions. Sometimes words or phrases are used in a **nonliteral**, or figurative way.

Literal: Let's <u>go take a hike</u> in the woods.

Nonliteral: "<u>Go take a hike</u>!" Anya yelled at her little brother. (What Anya means is "Go away.")

The chart below will help you understand some examples of nonliteral language, or figurative language.

Figurative Language	Definition	Examples
Idiom	Expression that cannot be understood from the meanings of its separate words but must be learned as a whole	Go take a hike! It's raining cats and dogs.
Simile	Comparison of two unlike things using the word *like* or *as*	The bed was <u>as soft as a kitten's fur.</u> Roger runs <u>like the wind.</u>
Metaphor	Comparison of unlike things in which one thing is said to be another thing	Kate is a busy bee. The lake was a shiny mirror reflecting the moon.
Personification	Giving living qualities to nonliving things	The flowers danced in the wind. The waves ran up and down the shore on watery feet.

Q: How do I figure out the meaning of **nonliteral,** or figurative language?

A: The best way to figure out the meaning of **nonliteral** language is to use the **context,** or the words and sentences that come before and after.

Example:

Lisa came to school with her clothes soaking wet. "It's <u>raining cats and dogs</u> outside," she said.

From the context, we understand that Lisa's clothes are soaking wet. We conclude that the phrase *raining cats and dogs* means that it's raining very hard.

 Try It

Directions: Read the following passage. Then answer the questions that follow.

My Red Boat

I folded red paper into a boat
And set it in the stream,
And it bobbed, bobbed, bobbed,
And danced about,
5 And I laughed in the bright sunbeams.

Slowly, slowly the water flowed
And carried the red boat with it,
And I followed along upon the shore
And danced about
10 And laughed in the bright sunbeams.

Then, quick as a wink, the current changed
And gave my red boat wings.
It flew along between the banks
And danced about
15 And sailed away in the bright sunbeams.

 GO ON

1 All of the following lines are meant to be taken literally EXCEPT—

   A *I folded red paper into a boat*

   B *And I laughed in the bright sunbeams.*

   C *Slowly, slowly the water flowed*

   D *And gave my red boat wings.*

2 Explain the meaning of lines 3 and 4 when the boat is described as dancing. Is this meant to be understood literally? If not, what kind of figure of speech is used?
(3 points)

_____

_____

_____

_____

_____

For **Example 1**, you must look at the lines given in the answer choices and evaluate whether they are meant to be taken **literally**. Choices A and B are referring to the child who makes the boat folding and laughing. Choice C describes the water flowing. All of these are things that actually happen. Choice D says the boat got wings. This doesn't happen literally. The correct answer is **choice D**, *And gave my red boat wings*.

For **Example 2**, you must explain the meaning of the phrase that describes the boat as dancing. You know that boats don't dance literally, so this is a figure of speech. However, what kind of figure of speech is it? By reviewing the chart on page 42, you see that dancing is something living things do, so this is an example of personification. From the **context** you understand that the meaning of the phrase is that the boat is moving up and down in the water so that it looks like it is dancing. A good response will answer all the parts of the written question.

Good: *Lines 3 and 4 are not meant to be taken literally. They contain a figure of speech called personification. The red boat looks like it is dancing in the water when it bobs up and down.*

A poor answer will not identify or explain the figure of speech.

Poor: *The lines mean the boat is dancing in the water. This could be literal dancing or a figure of speech like an idiom.*

3 Read these lines from the poem.

Then, quick as a wink, the current changed
And gave my red boat wings.

When the speaker says the current "gave my red boat wings," she means—

A there were red wings on the boat.
B the boat sailed very fast.
C the boat turned into a bird.
D the boat was just a dream.

4 What does the phrase "quick as a wink" mean? (3 points)

_____

_____

_____

_____

_____

5 The phrase "quick as a wink" is—

A an idiom.
B a simile.
C a metaphor.
D personification.

Structure and Point of View

Review the Standards (RL.3.5, RL.3.6)

- Explain how parts of a story build upon each other
- Explain the differences among your own, the narrator's, and a character's **point of view**

Q: How do parts of a work of literature build upon each other?

A: Most works of literature are broken down into smaller parts. A book is divided into chapters; a poem is broken into stanzas. Plays are made up of scenes and acts. These divisions help you think about smaller parts of a work so that you can better understand the entire work.

Q: What is **point of view**?

A: **Point of view** is the viewpoint from which the story is being told. The narrator is the person who is telling the story. Study the following chart.

Who Is Telling the Story?	Literature Term	Example	Things to Remember
A character in the story	First-person point of view	I adjusted my hat and slowly turned the creaky doorknob. "Here goes nothing," I thought as I entered the room.	Uses the pronouns *I, we, us.* You only know the thoughts and feelings of one character.
An outside narrator, not one of the characters in the story	Third-person point of view	Max adjusted his hat and slowly turned the creaky doorknob. He entered the room.	You may be able to learn the thoughts and feelings of multiple characters.

Remember that you as a reader also bring a point of view to the story. You may know things about the character or the events of the story that the character doesn't. A good reader understands the differences among his or her own, the narrator's, and a character's point of view.

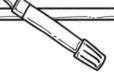

Try It

Directions: Read the following passage. Then answer the questions that follow.

The poem below tells the story of a giraffe named Ojo.

I Wish I Were . . .

A young giraffe named Ojo
Said to his mom and dad,
"I wish I were another animal.
I think that would make me glad."

"I want to be a lion
And be king of all I see."
They said, "If you were a lion,
You wouldn't eat leaves from trees."

"Then I want to be a hippo
Because rolling in mud is a treat."
They said, "If you were a hippo,
You wouldn't grow to 16 feet."

"Then I want to be a bug.
It might be fun to be a speck."
They said, "If you were a bug,
You wouldn't have a long, graceful neck."

"Then I want to be a crocodile
So I can swim with lots of power."
They said, "If you were a crocodile,
You couldn't run 30 miles per hour."

"Then I want to be a parrot
So I could sing a song."
They said, "If you were a parrot,
Your tongue wouldn't be 15 inches long."

"Then I want to be a snake
And have a tongue that I can flick."
They said, "If you were a snake,
You wouldn't have a powerful kick."

"Ojo, every living creature
Has something that makes it a 'star.'
You're a fine young giraffe—
Be happy with who you are!"

1 Which stanza of the poem introduces Ojo's problem?

  A stanza 1

  B stanza 2

  C stanza 3

  D stanza 8

2 Stanzas 2 through 7 are important because they—

  A describe the zoo where Ojo lives.

  B describe the animals that Ojo wants to be like.

  C describe Ojo's animal friends.

  D describe the animals that Ojo's parents want him to be like.

3 Who is narrating the events of the story?

  A Ojo

  B Ojo's mom

  C Ojo's dad

  D an outside narrator

4 Is the poem written in first-person or third-person point of view? Explain your answer using examples from the text. (3 points)

_____

_____

_____

_____

Example 1 asks you to think about how the stanzas of the poem relate to the overall story. In poetry, stanzas are indicated by a space between sets of lines. A close reading of the poem shows that stanza 1 introduces Ojo's problem of wanting to be like other animals, or **choice A**.

To answer **Example 2,** you must think about the purpose of stanzas 2 through 7. In these stanzas Ojo describes the animals he wishes he were like. In each stanza his parents explain the qualities that Ojo wouldn't have if he were that animal. The correct answer is **choice B**.

Example 3 asks you to think about who is narrating the poem, or who is telling the story. The poem uses the pronoun _I_, but only when a character is speaking. An outside narrator is telling the story, or **choice D**.

Example 4 asks you to think about which **point of view** the poem is written in—first-person or third-person. Since an outside narrator is telling the story, the story is written in third-person. Here is an example of a good answer.

Good: _The poem is written in third-person point of view. An outside narrator is telling the story of Ojo and his parents._

Directions: Read the following passage. Then answer the questions that follow.

Jack Fights Back

1   I've been having a lot of trouble with annoying people lately. My sister started it all. A couple of weeks ago she got into my things—again. When I got mad, she just seemed to make an even bigger mess! My mother said, "Jack, next time, just smile. Then she will stop."

2   Then, last week I invited my friend Hank over. He wanted to play with my army guys. But what Hank really wanted was to play with ALL my army guys while I just watched. That's not fair! My mom said, "Next time, just smile. Then Hank will let you play."

3   Yesterday I had to sit by Jamal at school. He always pokes me with his pencil. I got mad, and he just did it more. I told my mom and you know what she said? "Just smile and he will stop."

4   "Okay, okay, okay," I told her. "I will try it."

5   So today I tried it at school with Jamal. And guess what? It works!

5   Who is the narrator of the story?

   A   Jack's mom

   B   Jack's sister

   C   Jack

   D   Jamal

6   Because the story is written in first-person point of view,—

   A   we know the thoughts and feelings of every character.

   B   we know the thoughts and feelings of none of the characters.

   C   we know that thoughts and feelings of only one character.

   D   none of the above

7   Which of the following paragraphs explains how Jack's problem ends?

   A   paragraph 1

   B   paragraph 2

   C   paragraph 3

   D   paragraph 5

GO ON

8 Do you agree with Jack's mother's idea of how to deal with annoying people? Explain your point of view about his mother's advice to "just smile" when people do things you don't like. (3 points)

_____

_____

_____

_____

_____

Test-Taking Tips

1 To answer questions about figurative language, you must think about what is being compared. Think about how the two things are similar. Try to picture the image in your mind.

2 Point of view has to do with who is telling the story. If a character is telling the story, the story is in first-person point of view. If a narrator is telling the story, the story is in third-person point of view. Your point of view as a reader is different from the point of view of the characters or the narrator.

Go for it!

Unit Two Practice Test

Estimated time: 18 minutes

Directions: Read the following passage. Then answer the questions that follow.

In this selection, a group of friends is looking for information about something their friend's cat brought home. They think they might find something in a deserted house. Two of them decide to go in.

1 Ty went to the window. "Give me a boost," he said.

2 Toby bent over so Ty could stand on his back. Ty climbed on, reached up to the window, and pulled himself up.

3 The house was completely dark. Ty dragged himself through the window, and Gabe followed. Then they stood still for a few moments.

4 When their eyes finally got used to the dark, they could make out a doorway across the room. Ty began to creep toward it, and Gabe followed. Once there, they peeked through the doorway. A long, dark hallway seemed to lead to another door—a closed one.

5 They inched their way down the hall in the darkness and stopped at the door. The house itself seemed to be holding its breath. Not a sound could be heard. But both Ty and Gabe had the strange feeling that they were not alone.

6 After a few moments Ty carefully pushed the door open. Someone had nailed boards across all the windows. Very little light could steal its way in. But Ty could make out a shape in the corner. And it looked like a person! It was sitting very still on the floor with its back against the wall.

7 Ty was afraid to go closer. Finally, Gabe stuck his head in the doorway. He saw the shape too. Both boys stood still.

8 "Hello, boys," the body said.

9 Ty and Gabe screamed. Slamming the door shut, they ran back up the hall, through the other room, and dove out the window. Ty fell on Toby. Gabe fell on top of both of them.

10 Ty and Gabe jumped up and ran down the street. Toby limped after them.

11 When the boys saw Ben and Abe coming up the street, they stopped. They looked behind them. No one was there.

12 "What's wrong?" Ben asked. "You look like you've seen a ghost."

13 "Maybe," said Gabe, trying to catch his breath. His eyes were as big as quarters. Then he and Ty told the others what had happened.

14 "Well, the police are on their way," said Ben. "They'll see what's in that spooky old house."

GO ON

1   In paragraph 5, "The house itself seemed to be holding its breath" means—

   A the house was dark.

   B the house was very quiet and still.

   C the hallway was very cold and dark.

   D the house turned into a person.

2   Who is telling this story?

   A Ty

   B Gabe

   C someone who isn't in the story

   D a character in the story

3   Explain the meaning of "His eyes were as big as quarters" from paragraph 13. What kind of figure of speech is used? (3 points)

   _____

   _____

   _____

   _____

   _____

4   In which paragraph is the tension in the story the greatest?

   A paragraph 2

   B paragraph 6

   C paragraph 8

   D paragraph 14

5   The phrase "trying to catch his breath" from paragraph 13 is an example of—

   A personification.

   B an idiom.

   C a metaphor.

   D a simile.

Points Earned/Total = _____/7

Reading Literature Lesson 6

Illustrations

Review the Standard (RL.3.7)

• Explain how **illustrations** help you understand the story

Q: How do **illustrations** help me understand the meaning of the story?

A: Illustrations are pictures and photographs that the author includes with a story. Illustrations may give you more information about the characters' appearance or actions. If the book is set in a past time period, the pictures may help you understand the clothes, houses, and objects from the past or from different cultures.

 Try It

Directions: Read the following passage. Then answer the questions that follow.

Young Artist

I squirmed in my seat. It seemed as if class would last forever. As my teacher talked about poetry, I looked out the window. I could see the Japanese flag flying proudly in the breeze.

Just then, the bell rang. I sat up straighter in my seat. I put away my notebook and pencil. Now it was time for my favorite subject. Art!

Today we were going to study one of Japan's ancient crafts, origami. When you do origami, you take a square of paper and fold it into a beautiful shape. Most kids my age can fold a bird, a soldier's helmet, a flower, and other simple objects.

www.photos.com

GO ON

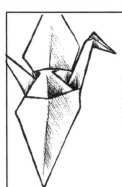

The art teacher entered the room. With the other students, I stood and bowed to show respect. Then I sat down with a big smile on my face. What would I learn to fold today?

1 How does the picture and the illustrations help you understand the story? (3 points)

_____

_____

_____

_____

_____

For **Example 1**, you must think about how the picture and the illustrations help you understand the story.

Good: *The illustrations and photo help the reader understand what origami is. They are helpful because some readers haven't done origami and don't know what it looks like. It helps the reader picture the type of artwork the speaker is doing.*

Poor: *The illustrations make the story more interesting and give the reader something to look at.*

◎ Try It On Your Own

2 The illustration best explains which of the following passages from the story?

A *I could see the Japanese flag flying proudly in the breeze.*

B *I put away my notebook and pencil.*

C *When you do origami, you take a square of paper and fold it into a beautiful shape.*

D *The art teacher entered the room. With the other students, I stood and bowed to show respect.*

3 Which of the following would be the most helpful for understanding the story?

A a picture of a classroom in Japan

B a map of Japan

C a picture of an American classroom

D a picture of a flower

Reading Literature
Lesson 7

Comparing and Contrasting Stories

Review the Standard (RL.3.9)

- **Compare** and **contrast theme**, **setting**, and **plots** of similar stories

Q: How do I **compare** and **contrast** the **theme**, **setting**, and **plots** of stories?

A: First, make sure you understand the terms *theme*, *setting*, and *plot*.

The **theme** of a story is the main idea or lesson about life.

The **setting** of a story is the time and place where the action takes place.

The **plot** of a story is the events that happen.

Comparing means showing how things are alike; *contrasting* means showing how things are different. It is helpful to use the Venn diagram below as you compare and contrast stories. The separate circles contain facts about the individual stories. These areas show how the stories are different. The overlapping area where the two circles meet shows how the stories are the same.

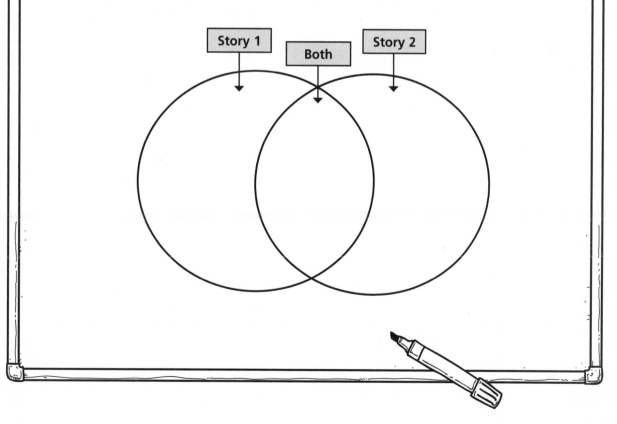

Story 1　　　Both　　　Story 2

GO ON

Directions: Read the following passages. Then answer the questions that follow.

The Sausage

1 An old woman was waiting for her husband to come home for dinner when she heard a knock on the door. Answering it, she saw a finely dressed lady.

2 "Please lend me your baking pan," the lady said. "My daughter is about to be married, and I must prepare for my guests."

3 Though she did not know the lady, the old woman quickly ran and got the pan. The lady took it, thanked the woman, and went away. When she returned two days later, she promised the woman three wishes, then quickly vanished.

4 The old woman was very excited and began to think what she should wish for. Maybe they could get a wonderful big farm, or a box full of money!

5 At that moment, though, the old woman was hungry. She had little food in the house, and she needed to prepare dinner for her husband.

6 "I wish I had that sausage I saw in the neighbor's kitchen!" the old woman said to herself. That very moment a big sausage appeared on the table.

7 When her husband came in, she told him about the wishes, and how she had just gotten them a sausage for dinner.

8 The husband became angry. "We could have anything in the world, and you wish for a sausage! I wish that sausage were sticking to your nose, you foolish woman!"

9 And guess what? The sausage immediately appeared on the woman's nose. Try as they might, they couldn't pull it off.

10 What could they do? They had one wish left. Would it be for riches—or to remove the sausage?

11 The husband made up his mind. "I wish my wife was rid of that sausage," he said.

12 And right away, the sausage was gone! The husband and wife celebrated as if they had just gotten a fortune.

The Three Wishes

1 Once there lived a poor woodsman in a great forest. One day he went out to cut wood and chose a big old oak tree. He was about to start cutting it into planks when he heard a sad cry. A spirit who lived in the tree was begging him not to cut it down.

2 The woodsman was amazed, but he told the spirit, "I will do as you ask."

3 The spirit was very grateful and said to the woodsman, "To show my thanks, I will give you any three wishes that you desire."

4 The spirit disappeared, and the woodsman started for home. He wasn't sure if the whole thing had been a dream.

5 When the woodsman arrived home, he was hungry and tired. No supper was ready, so he said, without thinking, "Oh, I wish I had some black pudding in front of me now."

6   No sooner had he spoken than a huge bowl of black pudding was before him. He and his wife were both amazed, and then he remembered what had happened in the forest.

7   His wife was very mad when she heard the story. "You are a fool," she said. "I wish the pudding was stuck to your nose." And, of course, right then it was. They pulled and pulled but could not get it off.

8   "What should I do now?" the woodsman said.

9   "It really doesn't look that bad," answered his wife.

10   So the woodsman made up his own mind and wished the pudding off his nose. His wife wasn't too happy, and she never got rich, but at least she had a good supper.

---

1   Both "The Sausage" and "The Three Wishes" are examples of—

   A poetry.
   B folktales.
   C nonfiction.
   D myths.

2   The finely dressed lady and the tree spirit are alike in that—

   A they grant the wishes to a character who helps them.
   B they are forced to grant the wishes.
   C they offer advice on how to use the wishes.
   D they are fairies.

3   Use the diagram below to help you compare and contrast the two stories.

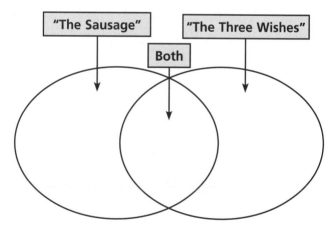

Which of the following would fit under the circle labeled "The Sausage"?

   A A spirit grants a woodsman three wishes.
   B The wife is upset by her husband's wish.
   C The husband wishes for black pudding.
   D A lady grants an old woman three wishes.

Example 1 asks you to **compare**, or to think about whether both passages are similar in their form. Both contain magical creatures who grant wishes, and in both stories the characters learn a lesson. Thus, the best answer is **choice B**, *folktales*.

GO ON

Example 2 asks you to think about how the characters who grant the wishes are alike. One is a spirit, and the other is a mysterious lady, so choice D is not correct. Choices B and C can also be eliminated because neither of these are true. However, both characters grant wishes after another character helps them. The answer is **choice A**.

To answer **Example 3**, think about how a Venn diagram is used to **compare** and **contrast** two stories. The question asks which information would go into the outer circle labeled "The Sausage." You need to find the information that is ONLY true of "The Sausage." By carefully reading the answer choices, you can see that the correct answer is **choice D**, *A lady grants an old woman three wishes.*

◎ Try It On Your Own

4 In both stories, the main character's last wish is for—

   A an item of food to be removed from a husband's or wife's face.

   B more wishes.

   C a bigger house.

   D more food and money.

5 Explain how the ending of the stories are alike and different. Use examples from the stories to support your answer. (3 points)

   _____

   _____

   _____

   _____

   _____

   _____

6 A central idea of both of these stories is—

   A strangers can't be trusted.

   B be careful what you wish for.

   C sometimes you can get rich easily.

   D husbands and wives don't always get along.

Test-Taking Tips

1 Use the pictures or illustrations in a story to help you understand the meaning in the story. Think about what ideas in the story the picture explains or gives more details about.

2 When comparing and contrasting two stories, think about how the characters, the plot, and the theme are the same or different. Also go back to the text and reread or underline important ideas.

Go for it!

Unit Three Practice Test

Estimated time: 25 minutes

Directions: Read the following passages. Then answer the questions that follow.

Little Red Riding Hood

1   Once upon a time, there was a little girl who lived with her mother. Her mother sewed her a cloak and hood. She used bright red cloth to make the cloak. The little girl wore the cloak everywhere she went. People began to call her Little Red Riding Hood.

2   Little Red Riding Hood had a grandmother who lived all alone. Her house was deep in the forest. One day Grandmother got sick. Little Red Riding Hood's mother fixed a basket of goodies. She told Little Red Riding Hood to take the food to her grandmother. Her mother warned her to go straight to her grandmother's house. She told her not to dally.

3   Just as Little Red Riding Hood entered the forest, a wolf came along. The wolf was big with long brown fur. The wolf asked Little Red Riding Hood what she was doing in the woods. She told the wolf that her grandmother was sick. She was on her way to visit her and take her some food. Then she continued on her way.

4   The wolf was a clever one. He dashed through the forest. He took a shortcut to Grandmother's house. He knocked on the door. When Grandmother asked who was there, the wolf said it was Little Red Riding Hood. As soon as Grandmother opened the door, the wolf gobbled her up whole. Then, the wolf put on some of Grandmother's clothing. The wolf climbed

GO ON

into bed to wait for the real Little Red Riding Hood to arrive.

5   Little Red Riding Hood entered her grandmother's house. It was very dark inside. The wolf had blown out the candles. Little Red Riding Hood reached out to touch her grandmother. "My, oh my, Grandmother, what big arms you have!" exclaimed Little Red Riding Hood.

6   "The better to hug you with," replied the wolf in his best Grandmother voice.

7   "My, oh my, Grandmother, what big ears you have!" exclaimed Little Red Riding Hood.

8   "The better to hear you with," replied the wolf.

9   "My, oh my, Grandmother, what big eyes you have!" exclaimed Little Red Riding Hood.

10   "The better to see you with," replied the wolf.

11   "My, oh my, Grandmother, what a big mouth you have!" exclaimed Little Red Riding Hood.

12   "The better to eat you with!" snarled the wolf. He leapt out of the bed and grabbed Little Red Riding Hood. A woodcutter happened to be passing by and heard the noise. He rushed into the house. The woodcutter killed the wolf and cut him open so that Grandmother could escape.

13   Little Red Riding Hood and her grandmother lived happily ever after. Everyone was thankful to the woodcutter!

Lon PoPo

1   One day, Mother decided to visit Grandmother on her birthday. She left her three children, Shang, Tao, and Paotze, at home. Mother told the children that she was going to spend the night at Grandmother's. "Lock the door and do not open it for anyone!" said Mother.

2   Soon after Mother left, along came a clever wolf. The wolf was dressed just like Grandmother and knocked on the door.

3   "Who's there?" asked the children.

4   "It is Grandmother, your PoPo," answered the wolf.

5   "But PoPo, our mother is on the way to visit you!" The children forgot what Mother told them about keeping the door locked. When they opened the door, the wolf burst inside. He quickly blew out the candles to make it dark. The wolf didn't want the children to see that he was really not their PoPo.

6   "It is already dark. Let us all go to bed," said the wolf.

7   The children and the wolf all climbed into bed. The children felt the wolf's bushy tail and claws right way. They figured out they had been tricked!

8   The children whispered to each other. "We have to have a plan. We don't want the wolf to know we've figured out he isn't our PoPo!"

9   The next morning, the sun reappeared. The children asked the wolf, "Have you ever eaten gingko nuts, PoPo? They are so tender, juicy, and delicious! We have a gingko tree right outside our door!"

10   The children went outside. They quickly climbed up the tree. They pretended to enjoy eating the nuts. Soon they invited the wolf to join them. But the wolf couldn't climb the tree. The children knew they could use their plan.

11   "PoPo, climb into the basket. We will pull you up," they called down to the wolf. The first time the wolf climbed into the basket, the children started to pull it up a little way. Then they dropped the basket with the wolf in it. They tried a second time. Again, they pulled it up a little way. Then they dropped the basket with the wolf in it again.

12   "Please, let us try one more time. We will all three pull this time!"

13   The third time, the children pulled the basket up higher and higher. When the wolf was almost at the top of the tree, the children let go of the rope. The wolf went crashing to the ground. The wolf hit the ground with such force that he died. The children climbed down the tree. They ran inside, locked the door, and waited until Mother returned.

14   When Mother came home, the children told her what had happened. "You must always listen to what I tell you," said Mother. "Still, I am thankful that I have three clever children who are smart enough to fool even a cunning wolf!"

1   The illustration for "Little Red Riding Hood" helps you understand—

A the character of the wolf.

B the time period in which the story is set.

C what the grandmother looks like.

D how the story ends.

2   Study this diagram about the wolves in the stories.

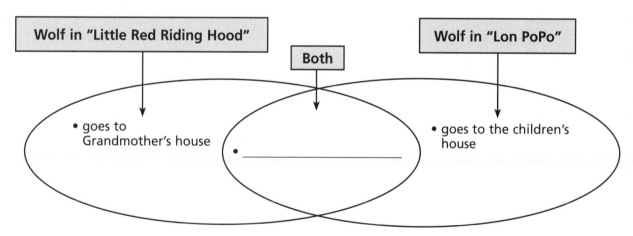

Which detail belongs in the center of this diagram?

A eats Grandmother

B dresses like Grandmother

C falls from a tree

D is killed by a woodcutter

3 How is the setting of the stories different? Explain your answer using examples from the stories. (3 points)

_____

_____

_____

_____

_____

_____

4 The children in "Lon PoPo" are different from Little Red Riding Hood because—

A they obey their mother's advice.

B they think the wolf is their grandmother.

C they don't have a grandmother.

D they catch the wolf themselves.

5 An important lesson of BOTH selections is—

A don't visit your grandmother alone.

B listen to what your mother says.

C don't be afraid of the dark.

D ask for help if you need it.

Points Earned/Total = _____ /7

Reading Informational Text Lesson 8

Ask and Answer Questions

Review the Standard (RI.3.1)

- Ask and answer questions about a **nonfiction** text
- Refer to the text as a basis for answers

Q: How can I use questions to help me understand an informational or **nonfiction** text?

A: Remember that reading an informational text such as a biography, history, or science text is different from reading a story. Your goal for reading **nonfiction** is usually to get information.

Before Reading Questions	During Reading Questions	After Reading Questions
• What do I think this passage is about? • What do I already know about the topic? • What questions do I think this passage will answer? • What do the title, introduction, or pictures tell me about what I will be reading?	• What have I learned so far? • What ideas/words are repeated throughout the passage? • What parts of the text do I not understand? (How can I better understand them?) • What can I learn from the pictures, captions, headers, and graphics?	• What questions were answered by the passage? • What was the main idea? • What connections can I make to other things I've read?

Q: Why should I refer to the text when answering questions?

A: You should always go back to the text when answering questions. Sometimes you will find the answer right in the passage. Other times you may be asked to give your opinion about something you read. When this is the case, you must make sure that your opinion is based upon specific facts from the text.

GO ON

Directions: Read the selection. Then answer the questions that follow.

A President's Pets

by Kathleen Muldoon

Calvin Coolidge was the thirtieth president of the United States. Some people thought he was shy. That's because he did not talk or smile very much. People nicknamed him Silent Cal.

But President Coolidge was not shy around animals. He and his family probably had more animals than any other first family.

Coolidge had several dogs. Rob Roy, a white collie, was his favorite. Mrs. Coolidge often dressed their dogs in dresses and hats.

President Coolidge also had cats. He liked Tiger best. Tiger was a stray that just showed up one day at the White House. He liked riding up and down on the White House elevator.

The Coolidges also had a mynah bird and two canaries, Nip and Tuck.

People around the world knew of the president's love of animals. They sent him a baby bear and two lion cubs. He also received a hippo, a bobcat, and an antelope. Coolidge gave these big animals to zoos.

But one day, he received a special gift from some friends in Mississippi. They sent him a furry raccoon. The president named her Rebecca. She became his favorite pet of all.

Rebecca was allowed to roam free. Sometimes visitors thought a wild animal had sneaked into the White House. They were surprised to learn that the raccoon was the president's pet!

At night, Rebecca slept outside. The president had a little house built just for her.

When he had time, Coolidge took Rebecca on walks. He kept her on a leash. Even on his busiest days, the president found time for Rebecca.

©Bettmann/CORBIS

Raccoon Photo: www.photos.com

1 Based upon the title and the pictures, the BEST question to ask before reading the passage would be—

    A Was the president allergic to cats?

    B Why are the pictures in black and white?

    C Who is the lady in the picture?

    D Did the president have a raccoon for a pet?

2 A good question to ask after reading the passage is—

    A What pets did President Coolidge have?

    B How did Coolidge become president?

    C Why was President Coolidge so unhappy?

    D How can I get a pet raccoon?

3 What details from the passage support the fact that Rebecca was the president's favorite pet? (3 points)

_____

_____

_____

_____

    Example 1 asks you to think about the best question to ask before reading the passage. The title hints that the topic is presidential pets, and there is also a picture of a man and woman with a dog and a picture of a raccoon. Thus, the best question to ask would be, *Did the president have a raccoon for a pet?,* or **choice D**.

    Example 2 asks you to think about a good question to ask after reading the passage. After reading the passage, you should ask questions that help you review the main idea. Since the main idea of the passage is about President Coolidge's pets, the best answer is **choice A**.

    When answering **Example 3**, you should go back and reread the paragraphs about Rebecca. Then find the details that support the idea that she was President Coolidge's favorite pet. These details should be included in your answer.

    Good: *Rebecca the raccoon was President Coolidge's favorite pet. She was allowed to roam free in the White House. The president built her a little house where she slept at night. Even when the president was busy, he made time to walk Rebecca on a leash.*

    A poor answer will not include specific details.

    Poor: *Rebecca was the president's favorite raccoon because she was a gift from some friends. The president really liked her.*

4 Coolidge was given the nickname "Silent Cal" because he—

   A did not talk or smile much.

   B talked only to animals.

   C did not want people to call him "president."

   D lost his voice after he became president.

5 The picture of President and Mrs. Coolidge supports all the following ideas from the text EXCEPT—

   A Coolidge has a white collie named Rob Roy.

   B President Coolidge was not shy around animals.

   C Mrs. Coolidge dressed their dogs in dresses and hats.

   D President Coolidge did not smile very much.

6 In what ways were President Coolidge's pets unusual? Give specific details from the text in your answer. (3 points)

_____

_____

_____

_____

_____

_____

_____

_____

_____

_____

_____

_____

_____

_____

_____

_____

Main Ideas and Supporting Details

Review the Standard (RI.3.2)

- Find the **main idea** of a text
- Recount the **key details** and how they support the main idea

Q: How do I determine the **main ideas** and **key details** of an informational text?

A: The **main idea** of a text is the main point, or what the text is mainly about. **Key details** are ideas and facts that support the main idea. The following web diagram can be helpful when trying to determine the main idea of a passage.

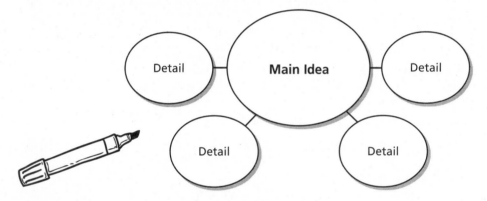

Q: How do **key details** support the **main idea**?

A: Supporting **details** give specific information about the **main idea**. Understanding the purpose of the passage, or why the passage was written, will help you predict the types of supporting details the author will use.

Purpose	Main Idea	Examples of Supporting Details
Explain the life of Martin Luther King Jr.	Martin Luther King Jr. was a leader in the fight for equal rights of African Americans.	He was born on January 15, 1929. In 1960, he was arrested while eating at a whites-only lunch counter in Atlanta. (Events)
Explain the steps for making tortillas	Making tortillas is not difficult when you follow these simple steps.	First, combine 2 cups *masa harina* and 2 cups of very warm water. Next, shape the dough into a small ball. (Steps)
Persuade people to eat more fruits and vegetables	Eating more fruits and vegetables will help you be healthier.	Fruits and vegetables are low in calories. Vegetables have high amounts of vitamins to prevent illness. (Reasons)

GO ON

Directions: Read the passage. Then answer the questions that follow.

You probably know that plants need water and soil in order to grow. Plants also need plenty of sunlight. You can prove that plants need sunlight by doing a simple experiment.

You will need three young seedlings in three different pots of soil. Beans or sunflowers are good choices for this experiment. Put one pot in a bright, sunny spot where it gets sun for at least half the day. Put another seedling in a dark corner of the same room. Put the third one in a closet that gets no light at all. Give the plants the same amount of water.

Measure the plants every two days. How tall have they grown? You will see that the plant that gets the most sunlight will grow the fastest. The plant in the far corner of the room will grow more slowly. The plant in the closet will grow very slowly. It may not grow at all. Can you figure out why?

1   What is the main idea of the passage?

   A Plants need water and soil in order to grow.

   B Measure the plants every few days.

   C An experiment can prove that plants need sunlight to grow.

   D Put the third plant in a closet that gets no light.

2   The main idea in this passage is supported by—

   A giving reasons why plants need the sun.

   B explaining an experiment that shows plants need sunlight.

   C giving facts about plants that need the most sunlight.

   D explaining how to grow a garden.

3   What are two key details that support the main idea of the passage? Write them below. (3 points)

   _____

   _____

   _____

   _____

Example 1 asks you to identify the **main idea**. The main idea of a passage is what the passage is mostly about. The first paragraph of the passage states, *"You can prove that plants need sunlight by doing a simple experiment."* The rest of the passage describes the experiment. **Choice C** is correct.

Example 2 asks you to think about how the **key details** support the main idea. The purpose of the passage is to explain how to conduct an experiment showing that plants need sunlight. The supporting details describe the steps in the experiment. The correct answer is **choice B**.

For **Example 3**, you must list two key details that support the main idea of the passage. You know the supporting details explain the experiment. Go back to the passage and find some details that explain the steps in the experiment. These should be important, or key, details, not minor ones.

Good: *Place three beans or sunflower seedlings in three pots of soil.*
   Put one pot in a sunny spot.

Poor: *Plants need plenty of sunlight.*
   Plants in the closet will grow slowly.

◎ Try It On Your Own

Directions: Read the passage.

When you visit national forests, ski resorts, and parks, don't be surprised to find an unusual sight. You just might see some goats busily munching away at plants. For many years, people have used goats for milk, meat, and wool. Now, forest and park managers have found another use for them. They use goats to control weeds.

Wildfires start easily in forest areas where there are many low plants and bushes. These plants become dry in the late summer and burn easily. Mowing helps control them, but it is expensive and dangerous. One spark from a mower can start a fire. Luckily, goats like to eat the low, dry plants. They can help keep the plants from growing out of control. Fewer dry plants and brush means fewer fires.

Another place goats help control plants is on the steep hills of ski resorts and forests. Poison oak and woody plants like to grow on hills. These plants are sometimes dangerous. Mowing on the steep hills is not possible. Chemicals work, but they often get into water that people use. Goats are the best answer. They like eating the unwanted plants. They even can eat poison oak without becoming sick.

Goats are also very quiet as they eat weeds. Visitors to peaceful parks don't like to hear loud mowers. The sight of goats quietly munching has been a welcome change at some parks.

Goats have quietly helped people for many years. Now, they have a new job. So on your next trip to a national park or forest, keep an eye out for these helpful creatures.

Directions: Study the web diagram below. Then answer the questions below.

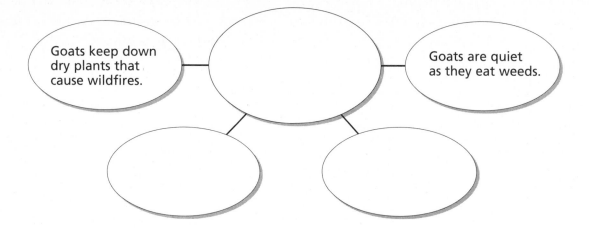

Goats keep down dry plants that cause wildfires.

Goats are quiet as they eat weeds.

4 Which sentence contains the main idea of the passage and belongs in the center circle of the diagram?

A For many years, people have used goats for milk, meat, and wool.

B Keep an eye out for these helpful creatures.

C Goats can eat poison oak without becoming sick.

D Forest and park managers use goats to control weeds.

5 Which sentence is a key detail and belongs in one of the outer circles of the diagram?

A Wildfires start easily in forest areas with many low plants and bushes.

B Chemicals hurt the water that people drink.

C Goats help control unwanted plants such as poison oak.

D You should visit national forests and parks.

6 Which of the following new sentences supports the main idea and would fit in one of the outer circles of the diagram?

A Goats have four legs and two horns.

B Mowers used in the national forests are very large.

C It costs very little to use goats for weed control.

D Goat meat is delicious.

Test-Taking Tips

1 As you read a passage, try to decide what the passage is mostly about. The main idea may be one sentence, or sometimes it may be two or more sentences.

2 Once you identify the main idea, you can check back for supporting details. Supporting details may give events, reasons, or steps depending upon the purpose of the passage.

Go for it!

Unit Four Practice Test

Directions: Read the following passage. Then answer the questions that follow.

1   Jesse sat in his usual shaded spot in Lafayette Park, across from the White House in Washington, D.C. This park had the largest number of gray squirrels in North America, and Jesse's project was to learn more about them.

2   The squirrel he called Sue ran down the tree, grabbed a nut Jesse had tossed her way, and used her strong teeth to crack it. Then, she rubbed it on the fur of her face to clean it before burying it. Later, in the winter, Sue would be able to find that nut and many more by following her own scent to it.

3   Outside Sue's territory, Tony, another of Jesse's favorites, was sharpening his teeth on the branch of a tree. Tony gnawed hard on the branch so his teeth would be clean and sharp. Jesse knew that a squirrel's teeth would grow six inches each year if they were not gnawed down.

4   Suddenly, Tony ran to the end of the branch and used his tail as a parachute to drop down to the branch of another tree. He had spotted Javier, a neighbor squirrel, trying to come into his territory. His tail quivered as he chattered at Javier. Javier used his tail to balance as he ran back to his own tree.

5   Jesse never tired of taking notes about the squirrels. He was going to have a great report for his teacher. Maybe his sister could come to watch tomorrow.

1   All the following are good questions to ask after reading the passage EXCEPT—

   A What did I learn about gray squirrels?

   B Where is Lafayette Park?

   C What other things have I read about gray squirrels?

   D What was the main idea of the passage?

2   Which sentence BEST describes what this story is mainly about?

   A Squirrels work hard all day long.

   B Tony entertains Jesse in Lafayette Park in Washington, D.C.

   C Jesse enjoys watching squirrels named Sue, Tony, and Javier.

   D Jesse watches gray squirrels to learn about them for a project.

3 Tony gnaws on the branch in order to—

   A drop down to another branch.

   B get to a nut.

   C clean and sharpen his teeth.

   D play a game with Javier.

4 Sue will be able to find her nut in the winter by—

   A following her tracks in the snow.

   B keeping Javier out of her territory.

   C keeping her teeth sharp.

   D following her own scent.

5 The web diagram below contains the main idea of paragraph 4.

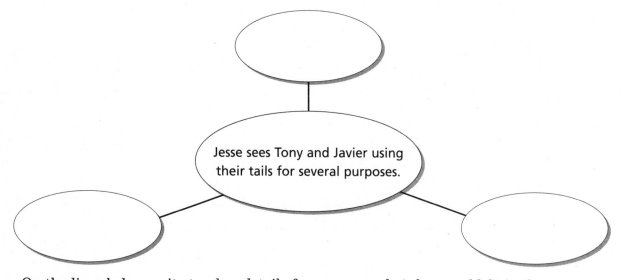

Jesse sees Tony and Javier using their tails for several purposes.

On the lines below, write two key details from paragraph 4 that would fit in the outer circles of the diagram. (2 points)

_____

_____

_____

_____

Points Earned/Total = _____ /6

Text Structures and Point of View

Review the Standards (RI.3.3, RI.3.6, RI.3.8)

- Describe the **relationship** between ideas in a text
- Describe the connection between sentences and paragraphs
- Explain the difference between your own **point of view** and the author's point of view

Q: How do I describe the **relationship** between ideas in text?

A: Information in nonfiction texts such as science and history books is often organized in one of the following ways:

Order	Key Terms
Sequence of events (Chronological order)	*first, second, next, then, finally, after, last*
Order of importance	*first, also, most importantly, another reason*
Cause and effect	*since, because, as a result of, resulting in*
Compare and contrast	*in the same way, similarly, like, unlike, different, on the other hand, however*

Look for the key terms in the chart as you read. They will help you understand the **relationship** between ideas in a text.

Q: How do I determine a writer's **point of view** in an informational text?

A: When we talk about **point of view** with nonfiction or informational types of writing, we are usually referring to a writer's opinion on the topic. In argumentative, or persuasive writing, the writer will give his opinion about a topic, then he will try to persuade you to agree with his opinion by giving reasons. To determine the writer's point of view, look for his opinions about the subject. As you read, think about how your point of view is the same or different from the writer's.

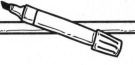

GO ON

Directions: Read the following passage. Then answer the questions that follow.

Helen Keller

1   In 1881, a baby girl named Helen Keller became very ill. She was only 19 months old. The scary sickness finally left her body, but it had caused terrible damage. Young Helen could no longer see or hear.

2   Helen's parents tried to help their daughter. It was very difficult. At that time, very few people knew how to help people like Helen. Helen and her parents could not communicate very well. To "speak," Helen could only giggle, kick, scratch, and scream. They all became very frustrated.

3   When Helen was almost seven, her parents found her a special teacher. The teacher, Anne Sullivan, came to the Keller house from Boston. Helen remembered this as one of the best days of her life. Miss Sullivan lived with Helen and tried to teach her how to communicate. She began by teaching her a new alphabet. She shaped letters with her hand. Helen felt the shapes with her own hands.

4   At first, Helen thought this was just a game. It took her a long time to understand that her teacher was making words that had meanings. When she did figure this out, it was thrilling. She wanted to know the name of everything. Finally, she had a way to communicate with others.

5   Helen had a strong hunger for learning. By the time she was 10 years old, she had learned to read Braille. Braille is a system of writing that uses raised dots on paper. Eventually, Helen also learned how to speak with her voice.

6   By the time Helen was a teenager, she was ready for college. Her teacher, Anne Sullivan, helped her during this time. In fact, Miss Sullivan spent the rest of her life helping Helen. They were hardly ever apart.

7   After Helen finished college, she wanted to help others. She was concerned about other people who were blind or deaf. People in poor countries concerned her the most. She wanted them to have the same opportunities that she had. She wrote books and articles. First, Helen wrote about her own life, hoping to inspire others. She asked wealthy people to give money to groups that helped the blind and deaf. She gave speeches in many countries. Her work earned her many medals and awards.

8   Helen Keller died in 1968. With help from a special teacher, she had lived a full and wonderful life.

1   The first paragraph explains that the result of Helen's sickness was that—

   A her parents were sad.

   B she lost her sight and her hearing.

   C she learned how to read Braille.

   D she died in 1968.

2 In what order does the writer present the information in the passage? Give examples of words that help you understand the order. (3 points)

_____

_____

_____

_____

3 Which of the following sentences from the passage gives the author's point of view, or her opinion, about Helen Keller?

A *Helen Keller became very ill.*

B *Young Helen could no longer see or hear.*

C *Helen Keller died in 1968.*

D *She had lived a full and wonderful life.*

Example 1 asks you to think about the **relationship** between ideas in the first paragraph. The question is asking about the result of Helen's illness. In the paragraph we learn that Helen became blind and deaf following her illenss. The correct answer is **choice B**, *she lost her sight and her hearing.*

To answer **Example 2**, you should think about how the information in the passage is organized. The passage is describing the events of Helen Keller's life so it is written in chronological order. A good answer will include this and will also give specific examples of time order words used in the passage.

Good: *The passage is written in order of the events of Helen Keller's life, or chronological order. The passage uses time words such as "In 1881," "At first," and "After Helen finished college."*

Poor: *The writer gives information about Helen Keller's life. He uses words that show the passing of time.*

Example 3 asks you to choose a sentence that gives the author's **point of view,** or opinion, about Helen Keller. An opinion is a personal perspective, not a fact. Only **choice D** gives an opinion about Helen Keller's life.

GO ON

4 Which paragraphs explain how Helen Keller learned to communicate?

    A paragraphs 1–2

    B paragraphs 3–4

    C paragraphs 5–6

    D paragraphs 7–8

5 Find two details from the passage that support the author's point of view that Helen Keller had a full and wonderful life. Write them on the lines below. (3 points)

_____

_____

_____

_____

_____

_____

6 What was the main problem that Helen Keller had to deal with in her life?

    A She did not like her teacher, Anne Sullivan.

    B She had trouble getting into college.

    C She had to learn how to communicate without her sight or hearing.

    D She didn't enjoy speaking in front of people.

Word Meanings

Review the Standards (RI.3.4, L.3.4, L.3.4.d, L.3.6)

- Find the meaning of words and phrases using context
- Use **glossaries** and **dictionaries**
- Understand and use academic words and phrases

Q: How can I figure out the meaning of unfamiliar words and phrases in a nonfiction text?

A: First, you should try to figure out the meaning based upon the **context**, or the words around the unknown word. These words will give hints to the unknown word's meaning. Often the sentence will contain a synonym (word that means the same) or an antonym (word that means the opposite) of the unfamiliar word.

Synonym: After dinner our dog <u>vanished</u>. He <u>disappeared</u> and we couldn't find him anywhere.

   Vanished means "disappeared."

Antonym: I was <u>anxious</u> about the test, but Dwayne was <u>not worried</u> at all.

Anxious means "worried."

Next, you should look up the unknown word in a **dictionary** or in the book's **glossary**. A glossary is a special dictionary that defines important words and terms used in the book. Sometimes glossary definitions are listed right next to the paragraph you are reading. Other times the word is marked in the text in boldface type, but you must go to the back of the book to find the glossary.

 Try It

Directions: Read the passage below. Then answer the questions that follow.

Gentle Giants

1   Elephants can eat a lot. An adult elephant can eat up to 500 pounds of food a day. Elephants don't eat other animals, though. They eat only plants.

2   Most elephants live in family units. An elephant family is made up of adult female elephants and their children. The oldest female <u>heads</u> the family. She is called the *matriarch*. She gets a lot of help leading the family from other adult females. Families usually have about 11 elephants, but they can have as few as 2 or as many as 29. Many families happily spend time with one another. Their members may touch trunks when they meet to say hello.

3   When a male elephant is about 12 years old, he leaves the family. He goes off on his own. He lives a <u>solitary</u> life. He may join other elephants for a while. However, he mainly lives by himself.

4   Elephants love water. They can drink 10 gallons at a time! When there is no water on the ground, they dig for it with their tusks. Then they use their trunks like straws to get the water. Elephants like to swim too. They are <u>excellent</u> swimmers and can swim underwater. They keep their trunks above the water so they can get air. Even baby elephants can swim.

5   Elephants need to take baths often. First, they suck water into their trunks. Then they spray the water out to give themselves a shower. The water keeps them <u>cool</u> in the warm weather. It also helps keep bugs off their backs. When water is hard to find, elephants will give themselves a dust bath. The dirt helps keep bugs off their <u>skin</u> too.

---

1   Read the meanings below for the word <u>head</u>.

> **head (hed)** *verb*
>   **1.** To be in charge of; lead. **2.** To turn in a certain direction. **3.** To place a heading on. **4.** To hit (a soccer ball) in the air with one's head.

Which meaning BEST fits the way <u>heads</u> is used in paragraph 2?

A definition 1

B definition 2

C definition 3

D definition 4

2   In paragraph 3, which words help you know what <u>solitary</u> means?

A *a male elephant*

B *about 12 years old*

C *goes off on his own*

D *may join other elephants*

3   What word means almost the same as <u>excellent</u> in paragraph 4?

A lazy

B bad

C funny

D good

Example 1 asks you to choose the **dictionary** meaning that best fits the way *heads* is used in the selection. The word *head* has more than one meaning. You must use **context** clues to find the correct one. Look carefully at the words and sentences around the target word. In paragraph 2, the sentence says that the oldest female heads the family. Later in the same paragraph, another sentence talks about the oldest female leading the family. Definition 1, *to be in charge of; lead,* makes the most sense. The other meanings do not fit. **Choice A is correct.**

Example 2 asks you to identify the context clues that help show the meaning of *solitary*. Paragraph 3 describes how a male elephant goes off on his own and mainly lives by himself. The word *solitary* must mean "alone." **Choice C**, *goes off on his own,* is the answer that gives clues to the meaning of *solitary*.

In **Example 3**, you must find the **word that means the same as** *excellent*. The word that has the closest meaning to *excellent* is *good*, **choice D**.

◎ Try It On Your Own

4 Which word means the OPPOSITE of <u>cool</u> in paragraph 5?

    A water

    B warm

    C cold

    D windy

5 Read this sentence from the passage.

The dirt helps keep bugs off their <u>skin</u> too.

Choose the sentence in which <u>skin</u> has a DIFFERENT meaning than in the sentence above.

    A Sunlight causes my <u>skin</u> to tan.

    B How did you <u>skin</u> your knee?

    C The elephant has tough <u>skin</u>.

    D Do you have freckles on your <u>skin</u>?

6 Based upon the meaning of the word <u>matriarch</u> in paragraph 2, which of the following uses the word correctly?

    A My mom is our family's <u>matriarch</u>.

    B The <u>matriarch</u> served our food at the restaurant last night.

    C As the <u>matriarch</u> of our family, my dad decides when I have to go to bed.

    D At the zoo, we watched a baby elephant use its <u>matriarchs</u> to pick up water and shoot it at the crowd.

Test-Taking Tips

1 Sometimes context clues aren't in the same sentence as the underlined word. Look at the sentences before and after the unknown word too.

2 Understanding how information is organized in a passage will help you understand what you are reading. Look for clue words to find causes and effects (*because, as a result*), reasons (*first, second, most importantly*), and events in chronological order (*first, the next day, then, afterward*).

3 As you read an informational text, think about the writer's point of view, or opinion. Then think about your own point of view. Do you agree with the writer's point of view? What are your reasons for agreeing or not agreeing?

Go for it!

Unit Five Practice Test

Estimated time: 20 minutes

Directions: Read the following passage. Then answer the questions that follow.

China's Great Wall

1   The Great Wall of China is an impressive sight. The longest wall ever built, it is more than 4000 miles long. That's longer than the distance from the East Coast to the West Coast of the United States!

2   The wall <u>runs</u> across the northern part of China. It goes through deserts, mountains, hills, and valleys. Parts of the wall are as much as 35 feet high and 25 feet across. In some parts, the top of the wall is almost as wide as a two-lane road.

3   The Great Wall took a long, long time to build. The work began in 221 B.C. At that time, several groups came together to form an empire, or kingdom. The first <u>emperor</u> of China wanted to protect his lands from enemies to the north. He gave the order to rebuild old walls and connect them to new ones. Over the next thousand years, the rulers of China added to and rebuilt the wall.

4   Different parts of the wall were made from different <u>materials</u>. What was used depended on what was on hand nearby. In the eastern part of the country, much of the wall was built with stone and bricks. In the western part, it was made mostly of earth and mud. Over the years, it took millions of workers to build the wall. Many people died while working on it.

5   Watchtowers were an important feature of the wall. These towers were up to 40 feet tall. They were built between 100 and 200 yards apart. Soldiers at each tower could look out over the nearby countryside. They would watch for invaders preparing to attack. If the soldiers saw anyone, they could send a signal to other towers. In this way, they could quickly warn others.

6   Today the wall looks different from the way it did long ago. Some parts made of earth hardly look like a wall at all. Time and weather have <u>worn</u> these parts away. However, other parts of the wall are in good shape.

7   The Great Wall of China is no longer used for protection. It is now a popular tourist site. Visitors from all over the world come to the wall every year. They can walk along the wall in many places. They can wonder about the time in which it was built. They also can appreciate the skill of the people who built it.

---

1   Read the meanings below for the word <u>run</u>.

> **run (rən)** *verb*
> **1.** To move on foot at a fast pace. **2.** To go from one stop to another along a regular route. **3.** To move around freely. **4.** To stretch across a space or area.

Which meaning BEST fits the way <u>runs</u> is used in paragraph 2?

A definition 1

B definition 2

C definition 3

D definition 4

2 Which word has almost the same meaning as <u>emperor</u> in paragraph 3?

   A ruler

   B visitor

   C soldier

   D word

3 In paragraph 4, which words help you know what <u>materials</u> means?

   A *stone and bricks*

   B *western part*

   C *made from*

   D *millions of workers*

4 Read the meanings below for the word <u>wear</u>.

> **wear (wâr)** *verb* wore, worn
> **1.** To have on or put on clothing. **2.** To exhibit: *wore* a frown.
> **3.** To damage by use or age. **4.** To tire out or exhaust.

Which meaning BEST fits the way <u>worn</u> is used in paragraph 6?

   A definition 1

   B definition 2

   C definition 3

   D definition 4

5 The content of the passage is organized by—

   A describing details about the wall.

   B explaining what visitors to the wall should look for.

   C giving reasons to visit the Great Wall of China.

   D telling the steps the builders used to create the wall.

6 Which paragraph explains what the wall is made of?

   A paragraph 2

   B paragraph 3

   C paragraph 4

   D paragraph 5

GO ON

7 In which sentence does the writer try to help the reader picture how long the Great Wall of China is?

A *The Great Wall of China is an impressive sight.*

B *The wall runs across the northern part of China.*

C *Parts of the wall are as much as 35 feet high and 25 feet across.*

D *That's longer than the distance from the East Coast to the West Coast of the United States!*

8 What is the writer's opinion, or point of view, about the Great Wall of China? What details from the text support the writer's opinion? Do you agree with the writer's opinion? (5 points)

_____

_____

_____

_____

_____

_____

_____

_____

_____

_____

_____

_____

_____

_____

_____

_____

_____

_____

Points Earned/Total = _____/12

Text Features and Illustrations

Review the Standards (RI.3.5, RI.3.7)

- Use **text features** and **search tools**
- Use information from illustrations, maps, and photographs to understand a text

Q: What are **text features**?

A: Text features include pictures, diagrams, charts, and graphs. Think about how they fit with what you read in the text. Other types of text features used in informational text are tables of content, indexes, and headings. A table of contents lists the chapters in the book. The index is found in the back of a book and lists the topics found in the book along with the page numbers where you can find the information. Headings are **key words** and phrases that identify the main ideas found in that section of the book.

Q: What are **search tools**?

A: Search tools help you find information within a Web site or an e-book. Study the sample below.

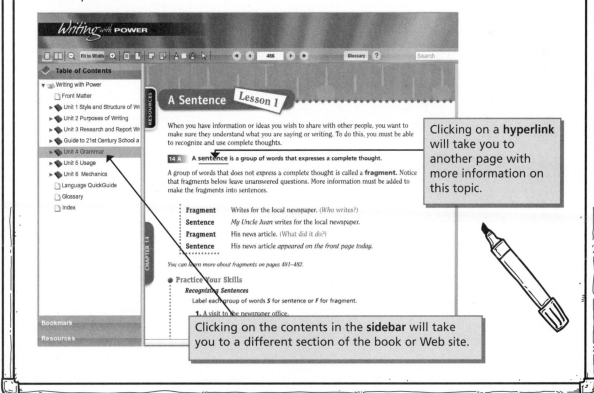

Clicking on a **hyperlink** will take you to another page with more information on this topic.

Clicking on the contents in the **sidebar** will take you to a different section of the book or Web site.

GO ON

Directions: Read the selection. Then answer the questions that follow.

Insect-Eating Plants

Most plants make their own food by mixing air, water, and nutrients from the soil with sunlight. One of the important nutrients plants need in order to survive is nitrogen. Nitrogen is usually found in soil. But some plants live where the soil contains very little nitrogen. These plants get the nitrogen they need from another source—insects. There are several types of plants that eat insects. Each kind has its own special way of trapping and "eating" bugs.

Pitcher Plant

The pitcher plant has a simple way to trap bugs. This plant gets its name because it looks like a pitcher. The top leaves are wide and form a spout. The lower leaves are folded together to form a tube where water collects when it rains. The plant attracts bugs with a sweet smell from nectar glands. When an insect lands on the plant, thick hairs keep it from flying away. The insect then slides down the tube and drowns in the water at the bottom. Then the plant digests the insect. Pitcher plants have red or yellow flowers. They may look pretty, but they are dangerous for bugs.

Butterwort Plant

The butterwort plant has another clever way to catch bugs. The leaves of this common plant make a sticky substance that bugs are drawn to. When an insect lands on one of the sticky leaves, the edges curl in and trap the insect. The insect dies, and then the plant digests it.

The Venus flytrap can eat flies, ants, crickets, and other small insects.

www.Photos.com

Venus Flytrap

The Venus flytrap is another unusual plant that eats insects. This plant has white flowers and green jawlike leaves. The leaves have two sides that are hinged together. Thin bristles stick out of each side like delicate teeth. But the flytrap does not "chew" its food. There are small "trigger" hairs on the inside of each leaf. When an insect lands on the hairs of an open leaf, the two sides close, trapping the bug inside. The plant then uses special fluids in the leaf to help digest the bug. After the plant finishes absorbing the nitrogen from the insect, the leaf opens up to catch another one. The leaf of a Venus flytrap dies after eating several insects.

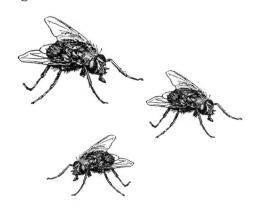

1 Which title or heading tells what the selection is mostly about?

   A Insect-Eating Plants

   B Pitcher Plant

   C Butterwort Plant

   D Venus Flytrap

2 According to the caption, the Venus flytrap can eat—

   A nectar.

   B mice.

   C honey.

   D ants.

Directions: Use the table of contents and index to answer questions 3 and 4.

Table of Contents

Index

---

3 In what chapter does "Insect-Eating Plants" belong?

  A Chapter 1

  B Chapter 2

  C Chapter 3

  D Chapter 5

4 Which page should you read to find out what a *node* is?

  A page 17

  B page 18

  C page 19

  D page 20

    Example 1 tests your knowledge of **titles** and **headings**. The use of titles and headings is a way to organize a text. A title gives the main idea of a text. A heading gives the main idea of a section in the text. Example 1 asks about the main idea of the text, so the title *Insect-Eating Plants*, **choice A**, is correct. Choices B, C, and D are headings. Texts are also organized by **paragraphs**. Each paragraph tells about an important idea that supports the main idea of the text.

    Example 2 asks about a caption. A caption is printed under an illustration or photograph and tells about the picture. According to the caption, the Venus flytrap can eat *ants*. **Choice D** is the correct answer.

A **table of contents** lists the chapters and other parts of a book and gives page numbers for them. Each chapter title tells the main idea of that chapter. **Example 3** asks which chapter "Insect-Eating Plants" belongs in. Since this selection tells about kinds of plants, it would best fit in Chapter 2, "Kinds of Plants." **Choice B** is correct.

Example 4 asks about an **index**. An index lists the topics in a book in alphabetical order. It gives the page numbers where each topic is found in the book. To answer this question, look in the index for the topic "node." The index tells you that *node* is found on page 18. **Choice B** is correct.

◎ Try It On Your Own

Directions: Study the graph and the Web page. Then answer the questions that follow.

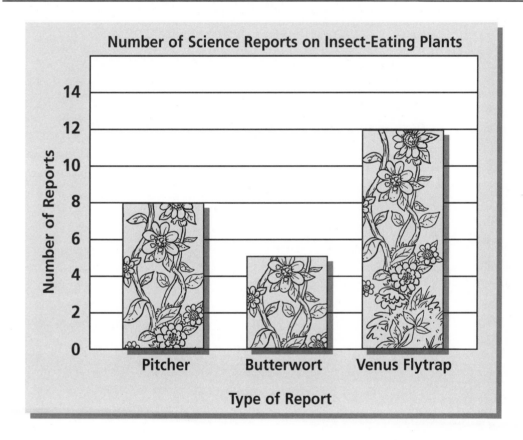

Number of Science Reports on Insect-Eating Plants

5 How many students wrote reports on the butterwort plant?

   A 1   **C** 8

   B 5   **D** 12

6 How many total reports were turned in?

   A 3   **C** 20

   B 12   **D** 25

Address: http://www.carnivorousplants.com/venusflytrap.php   Go ➡

⭑ Home   **⭑ Carnivorous Plants**   **⭑ Pet Owners**   **⭑ Plant Care**   **⭑ About Us**

Carnivorous Plants
- ◎ Venus Flytrap
- ◎ Sundew
- ◎ Nepenthes
- ◎ Pitcher Plant
- ◎ Terrariums
- ◎ Seed Kits, Accessories

Venus Flytrap
- ◎ Overview
- ◎ Feeding & Care
- ◎ Picture Gallery
- ◎ Buy

Venus flytraps make great pets. They will eat anything that gets trapped in their fast jaws, including bugs, flies, and insects. When the sensors inside their mouth are tripped, their jaws snap shut. It's amazing to watch. Venus flytraps are safe for children and not hard to care for.

Flytraps were originally found in the United States along the coastlines of North Carolina, so they like warmer temperatures. Many people keep their pet Venus flytrap in a **terrarium** so the temperature stays the same all the time. Our Venus flytrap **care instructions** and **care accessories**, packaged with dried flies, will keep your pet healthy and happy.

Your Venus flytrap comes in a package ready to go. Just make sure someone is home to open the package right away.

Order yours today!

---

7 Clicking on the sidebar will take you to all of the following topics EXCEPT—

A Sundew.

B Pitcher Plant.

C Accessories.

D Care Instructions.

8 Which of the following words in the text is a hyperlink, or will take you to another page with more information on the topic?

A Venus flytrap

B United States

C terrarium

D dried flies

Reading Informational Text Lesson 13

Comparing and Contrasting Texts

Review the Standard (RI.3.9)

• **Compare** and **contrast** two texts on the same topic

Q: How do I compare and contrast two texts on the same topic?

A: Remember that **comparing** means showing how two things are the same and **contrasting** means showing how two things are different. For each text, ask yourself the following questions:

• Why did the author write this?

• What is the main idea?

• What ideas are found in both texts?

• What ideas are found in one of the texts but not the other?

Use the following diagram to help you show how two texts are the same and different.

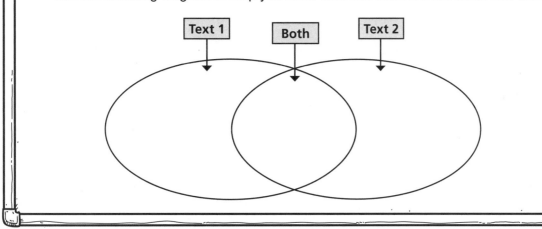

 Try It

Directions: Read the following passages. Then answer the questions that follow.

An Amazing Animal

1 Dr. Penny Patterson remembers when she first met Koko the gorilla. It was a foggy July morning in 1972. Koko lived in a nursery at a zoo. When Dr. Patterson walked into the nursery, Koko climbed right into her arms. The baby gorilla watched Dr. Patterson's hands as they said "Hello" in sign language. Koko answered by patting her own head.

2 Dr. Patterson was interested in trying to communicate with gorillas. She already knew that gorillas sometimes use hand signs to "talk" to other gorillas. Could she teach a gorilla to use American Sign Language to "talk" to people? She wanted to try.

3   To teach Koko a word, Dr. Patterson first made the sign herself. She did this while saying the word. Then she formed Koko's hands into the shape of the sign. It took baby Koko only two weeks to learn the signs for words like *food* and *drink*. Other words took longer.

4   It wasn't always easy for Koko to learn new words. She had trouble making some signs. Gorilla hands are shaped differently than human hands. Koko had to change some signs so that she could make them with her gorilla hands.

5   Koko is now over 30 years old. She knows over 1000 signs. And she is still showing Dr. Patterson how smart she is. Sometimes Koko can describe an object she's never seen before. When she first saw a mask, she signed "eye hat."

6   Dr. Patterson has written books about Koko. She also helps other people talk to Koko. With Dr. Patterson's help, Koko can even chat online! Dr. Patterson wants the whole world to learn about this amazing animal.

Talking to Dolphins

1   When you want to know what someone is thinking, you can always ask. But what if you want to know what a dolphin is thinking?

2   Dr. Ken Marten is a scientist who is very curious about dolphins. So curious, he's trying to get them to "talk" to him. He's inventing a special language that he hopes people and dolphins can share.

3   Dr. Marten began his experiment by studying the whistles dolphins make on their own. Then he started inventing new whistles on a computer. Each of his whistles has a simple meaning, such as "ball."

4   Dr. Marten teaches the dolphins his new whistles. One dolphin Dr. Marten works with is named Maui. To teach Maui the whistle for a word like "ball," Dr. Marten plays the whistle. At the same time, he holds up a real ball. Sometimes he uses a small dolphin puppet to add some fun. Maui eventually repeats Dr. Marten's whistle, but changes it slightly. Dr. Marten then uses Maui's whistle as the new whistle for "ball."

5   To make learning even more fun, Dr. Marten also uses a computer game. A special underwater touch screen shows four objects. He plays a whistle for one of the objects. If Dr. Marten plays the whistle for "bucket," he wants Maui to touch the picture of the bucket. If Maui does—bingo! The bucket dances around on the screen. All the dolphins seem to enjoy this game.

6   Dr. Marten thinks Maui and the other dolphins are learning the new whistle language. He writes reports about them for other people to read on the Internet. Dr. Marten wants everyone to know how much dolphins can learn.

1   The main purpose of both selections is to—

   A tell about how animals are learning to communicate with humans.

   B show that scientists love working with animals.

   C describe made-up stories about talking animals.

   D explain why some animals are more intelligent than others.

2 Use the Venn diagram to answer the following questions.

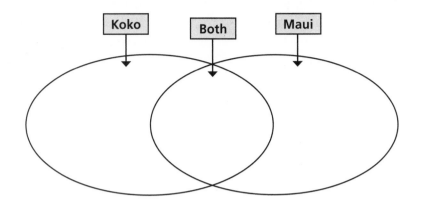

Which of the following would go in the right circle under **Maui**?

A communicates using hand signs

B communicates using whistles

C can describe an object

D can chat online

3 Based upon your reading of the passages, explain how both Koko and Maui are using computers in their communication. Write your answer on the lines below. (5 points)

_____

_____

_____

_____

_____

_____

For **Example 1,** you must think about how the purpose of both selections is the same. Remember that the purpose of a passage is why it was written. Choice C is incorrect because the passages are true, or nonfiction. Choice D is not correct, because neither article tries to support the idea that gorillas or dolphins are more intelligent. Between choices A and B, *tell about how animals are learning to communicate with humans* is the best, since both of the articles describe how they are learning to communicate. The correct answer is **choice A.**

Examples 2 and **3** ask you to use a diagram to **compare** and **contrast** the two passages. For **Example 2**, you need think about the facts that are only true of Maui the dolphin and would fit under the circle on the right. If you review "Talking to Dolphins," you will find that the only answer that is true of Maui is *communicates using whistles*, or **choice B.**

Example 3 asks you to think about how both Koko and Maui use computers to communicate. Paragraph 6 of "An Amazing Animal" says that Koko uses computers to chat online. Paragraph 5 of "Talking to Dolphins" describes how Maui uses a computer game to respond to whistles Dr. Marten makes. Here is an example of a good answer:

Good: *Both Koko and Maui use computers to communicate. Koko is able to chat online with other people. Maui plays a game where he touches a picture of an object on a computer screen when Dr. Marten plays a whistle for that object.*

A poor answer will not give specific examples of how Koko and Maui use computers or will give incorrect information.

Poor: *Koko can play computer games. Maui can use the Internet.*

◎ Try It On Your Own

4   Look at the chart below comparing the two stories. Fill in the blank box with a detail from "Talking to Dolphins" that makes the most sense. (2 points)

An Amazing Animal	Talking to Dolphins
Gorillas use hand signs with other gorillas.	
Dr. Patterson wondered if people could "talk" to gorillas using American Sign Language.	Dr. Marten wondered if people could "talk" to dolphins using new whistles.
Koko learns the signs, but sometimes has to change them slightly.	Maui repeats Dr. Marten's new whistles, but changes them slightly.

5   Why do Dr. Patterson and Dr. Marten write books and reports about their experiments? (3 points)

_____

_____

_____

Test-Taking Tips

1 Before answering questions, be sure to read the entire selection, including titles, headings, captions, and any graphic organizers, such as charts. Think about how they give more information about the topic.

2 Watch for keywords printed in **bold** or *italic* font—this shows that the words are important. Bold words are usually defined in a glossary.

Go for it!

© **Perfection Learning®** **No reproduction permitted.**

Unit Six Practice Test

Estimated time: 25 minutes

Directions: Read the following selection. Then answer the questions that follow.

Types of Volcanoes

1 A volcano is a mound or mountain formed around a **vent** in the earth's crust. Lava, steam, ash, and other materials **erupt** from this vent. Some volcanoes erupt often, and others rarely erupt.

2 Scientists classify three main types of volcanoes. They are composite, shield, and cinder-cone volcanoes. Though all three share similarities, they also have important differences. Each type of volcano is defined by a special characteristic.

Composite Volcanoes

3 The *composite volcano* is tall and has a **crater** at the top. There is a **central** vent or several vents where the lava comes out. Eruptions are forceful, sending lava shooting into the air. Composite volcanoes are made up of a *composite*, or combination, of different materials. Lava and rock fragments are two common materials.

4 Composite volcanoes are sometimes called *strato volcanoes*. Examples of composite volcanoes are Mount St. Helens in the United States and Mount Fuji in Japan.

Shield Volcanoes

5 The *shield volcano* is flatter on top than the composite volcano. The shield volcano's sides slope gently, like a warrior's shield. When this volcano erupts, the lava flows like an overflowing sink down the sides of the volcano.

6 The islands of Hawaii are a chain of shield volcanoes.

Cinder-Cone Volcanoes

7 The *cinder-cone volcano* has steeply sloped sides, like a cone. It has a bowl-shaped crater at the top. When it erupts, lava shoots into the air. The lava breaks up into little pieces called *cinders*.

8 A well-known cinder-cone volcano is Parícutin in Mexico.

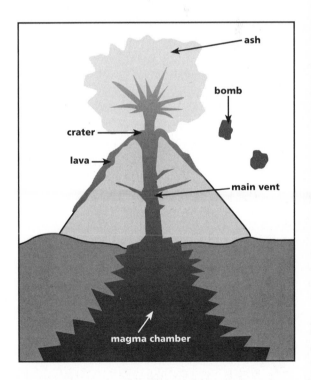

GO ON

1 Which tells what the passage is mostly about?

 A the title "Types of Volcanoes"

 B the heading "Composite Volcanoes"

 C the heading "Shield Volcanoes"

 D the heading "Cinder-Cone Volcanoes"

2 An important term in paragraph 5 is—

 A shield volcano.

 B composite volcano.

 C lava.

 D overflowing sink.

3 According to the diagram, when a volcano erupts, magma travels from the—

 A crater to the magma chamber.

 B crater to the main vent.

 C lava to the ash.

 D magma chamber to the main vent.

4 The diagram is of a—

 A composite volcano.

 B shield volcano.

 C cinder-cone volcano.

 D Hawaiian volcano.

5 Study the glossary.

Glossary

central	in the center or middle
crater	a bowl-shaped pit at the top of a volcano
erupt	to burst out suddenly
vent	an opening that air, smoke, or other matter comes out of

According to the glossary, a **crater** is found—

 A in the center of a volcano.

 B at the top of a volcano.

 C at the bottom of a volcano.

 D where the lava gathers.

Directions: Use the table of contents and index to answer questions 6 and 7.

Table of Contents

Index

6 Which chapter would most likely tell how to make a model of a volcano?

A Chapter 1   **C** Chapter 3

B Chapter 2   **D** Chapter 4

7 To read about a lava fountain, you should turn to page—

A 3.   **C** 27.

B 5.   **D** 33.

Directions: Use both "Types of Volcanoes" and "Hawaiian Volcanoes" to answer the following questions.

Hawaiian Volcanoes

You may know that Hawaii is made up of a chain of islands in the Pacific Ocean, but did you know that the islands are actually volcanoes? Scientists believe that these volcanoes began to form more than 70 million years ago. Each Hawaiian island is made up of one or more shield volcanoes, which first erupted on the sea floor. After many, many eruptions the volcanoes reached above the ocean's surface.

Today, Hawaii has three active volcanoes. Two of these are located in Hawaii Volcanoes National Park on Hawaii's Big Island. Mauna Loa last erupted in 1984, and Kilauea has been continuously erupting since 1983. The third volcano, Loihi, is located underwater off the southern coast of Hawaii's Big Island. In another 250,000 years, Loihi may break the surface of the ocean and add a ninth island to Hawaii's chain.

8 Both passages give information about—

    A composite volcanoes.

    B volcanoes in Hawaii.

    C cinder-cone volcanoes.

    D types of volcanoes.

9 What detail is given in the second passage that is not included in the first passage?

    A Shield volcanoes are flat on top.

    B The Hawaiian islands are shield volcanoes.

    C The lava flows down the sides of the volcano.

    D Hawaiian volcanoes are still erupting.

10 Rewrite paragraph 6 of "Types of Volcanoes" so that it includes more specific details from "Hawaiian Volcanoes." (3 points)

STOP

Points Earned/Total = _____/12

Language
Lesson
14

Nouns

Review the Standards (L.3.1.a, L.3.1.b, L.3.1.c)
- Explain the function of **nouns**
- Form and use **regular** and **irregular plural** nouns
- Use **abstract** nouns

Q: What are **nouns**?

A: Nouns are a part of speech that name people, places, and things.

Example: Tim fell on the **playground** and skinned his **knee**.

Tim, **playground**, and **knee** are all nouns.

Q: How do I make nouns **plural**?

A: When a noun means only one, it is singular. When a noun means more than one, it is **plural**. The **regular** way of making a noun plural is to add an *s* on the end.

Example: Singular = kitten   Plural = kittens

When a noun ends in *s, z, x, sh,* and *ch*, add *-es* to make it plural.

Singular	Plural
dress	dresses
box	boxes
dish	dishes
church	churches

Some nouns change form when they become plural. The following chart shows a few **irregular** nouns.

Singular	Plural
man	men
child	children
woman	women
ox	oxen

Q: What are **abstract** nouns?

A: Abstract nouns name a quality, idea, or concept that cannot be seen or touched. Examples include *love, freedom, childhood, happiness,* and *courage.*

In early **childhood**, Helen Keller was struck with a disease that left her blind and deaf.

GO ON

Try It

Directions: Read the following questions. Then choose the best answer.

---

1 Which underlined word from the sentence is a noun?

<u>In</u> August the <u>animals</u> <u>could</u> not <u>find</u> <u>any</u> food.

A In
B animals
C find
D any

2 Which of the following plural nouns is correct?

A snowmans
B wishs
C boxs
D bunches

3 Use the word *love* as an abstract noun in a sentence. (1 point)

_____

_____

_____

Example 1 asks you to identify the **noun** in the sentence. Remember that a noun names a person, place, or thing. Animals are things, so the correct answer is **choice B**.

For **Example 2**, you must think about the rules for making nouns **plural**. Choices B and C are incorrect because if a word ends in *s, x, z, sh,* or *ch,* you must add *–es* to the end to make it plural. The plural of *snowman* is *snowmen,* so choice A is incorrect. The correct answer is **choice D**, *bunches*.

Example 3 asks you to use *love* as an **abstract noun** in a sentence. Be careful to use *love* as a noun, not a verb.

Correct: *Because of her <u>love</u> for animals, she volunteers at an animal shelter.*
Incorrect: *I <u>love</u> animals, especially dogs and cats.*

4 Which underlined word from the sentence is a noun?

There had been little rain, and the grass, small plants, and leaves were scarce.

A There

B little

C rain

D scarce

5 Write another noun from the sentence above on the line below. (1 point)

_____

_____

6 Which of the following plural nouns is correct?

A oxes

B buzzs

C mouses

D teeth

7 In which of the following sentences is the underlined word NOT an abstract noun?

A He was awarded a medal for bravery.

B His fear kept him from trying out for the team.

C Freedom is worth fighting for.

D The happy dog played in the yard.

Language Lesson 15

Pronouns

Review the Standards (L.3.1.a, L.3.1.f)

- Explain the function of **pronouns**
- Make pronouns and their **antecedents agree**

Q: What are **pronouns**?

A: Pronouns are a part of speech that take the place of a noun. Examples of pronouns are *I, we, she, they, us, yours,* and *its.*

Examples: <u>Mary</u> is my sister.

<u>She</u> is my sister.

Megan gave <u>Megan's</u> friend a book.

Megan gave <u>her</u> friend a book.

Q: How do I make pronouns and **antecedents** agree?

A: Pronouns must agree with the noun to which they refer, or their antecedent. They must be the same in number (singular or plural) and gender (male or female).

Incorrect agreement: <u>Robbie and Lau</u> ate <u>his</u> lunches in less than 10 minutes.

His is singular, but *Robbie and Lau* are plural. They do not agree in number.

Correct agreement: <u>Robbie and Lau</u> ate <u>their</u> lunches in less than 10 minutes.

Incorrect agreement: My <u>Aunt Jenny</u> lost <u>its</u> way in the storm.

Its is used to refer to objects and animals when the sex is unknown. We know Aunt Jenny is a woman, so *her* is correct.

Correct agreement: My <u>Aunt Jenny</u> lost <u>her</u> way in the storm.

Try It

Directions: Read the following questions. Then choose the best answer.

1 In the sentence below, which of the underlined words is a pronoun?

That <u>morning</u>, a <u>mother</u> opossum carrying <u>her</u> babies on her <u>back</u> had scurried across the yard.

A morning **C** her
B mother **D** back

2 Which pronoun below fits in the blank?

The blue jay and the cardinal didn't have strength to fight over the little puddle of water that _____ found in the early morning.

A he   **C** they

B it   **D** their

For **Example 1**, you must decide which word is a **pronoun**. Remember that pronouns take the place of nouns. The correct answer is *her*, **choice C**.

For **Example 2**, you must choose the correct pronoun that fits in the sentence. First, you should find the **antecedents**—the blue jay and the cardinal. This means you need a plural pronoun, so you can cross out choices A and B. Next read the sentence, inserting the final two choices. **Choice C**, *they*, is correct.

◎ Try It On Your Own

Directions: Read the passage, and then answer the questions that follow.

Alexis was so excited for her trip. She loved to read about history, and his dream had always been to visit Washington, D.C. She was excited to see D.C. and its museums and memorials.

3 All of the following are pronouns used the passage EXCEPT—

A Alexis.   **C** his.

B she.   **D** its.

4 What is the antecedent of the pronoun *her* in the sentence below?

Alexis was so excited for her trip.

A Alexis   **C** excited

B was   **D** trip

5 The following sentence contains a pronoun error.

Since Anna loved history, his dream had always been to visit Washington, D.C.

Rewrite the sentence so that the pronoun is correct.

_____

_____

_____

GO ON ⇨

Verbs

Review the Standards (L.3.1.a, L.3.1.d, L.3.1.e, L.3.1.f)
- Explain the function of **verbs**
- Form and use **regular** and **irregular** verbs
- Form and use simple verb **tenses**
- Make subjects and their verbs **agree**

Q: What are **verbs**?

A: Verbs show action or being.

 Action: Martha <u>runs</u> with her dog.

 Being: Those houses <u>are</u> big.

Q: What is verb **tense**?

A: Verb **tense** shows time. Is the action/being taking place right now? Did it already take place? Will it take place in the future?

 The **regular** way to show past tense is to add -ed to a verb.

 Examples: walk, walked   add, added   stop, stopped

 However, some verbs are **irregular**. This means they change their form to show past tense.

 Examples: eat, ate   sing, sang   buy, bought

 To show future tense, *will* is often added to the present tense.

 Examples: I <u>will walk</u> to school tomorrow.

 My mom <u>will buy</u> me a new video game after my birthday.

Q: How do I make subjects and verbs **agree**?

A: Subjects and verbs must agree in number. If the subject is only one (singular), then the verb must singular. If the subject is more than one (plural), then the verb must be plural. Remember that to make a verb singular, you often add an -s or -es.

 Examples: The student sings a solo in Spanish. (*Student* and *sings* are both singular.)

 Your children play on the playground during recess. (*Children* and *play* are both plural.)

➡ Try It

Directions: Read the following questions. Then choose the best answer.

1 Tomorrow, I ___ to the park.

 A goed
 B will go
 C going
 D went

2 Which sentence is written correctly?

 A The lions likes the warm sunlight.
 B The lions is liking the warm sunlight.
 C The lions does like the warm sunlight.
 D The lions like the warm sunlight.

3 Which word in the sentence is a verb?

 The flood waters rose over the dams.

 A flood
 B waters
 C rose
 D over

Example 1 asks you to choose the correct form of the verb *go*. *Go* is an **irregular** verb; you know that *goed* isn't correct. *Went* is the **past tense**. A **future** tense verb is needed. The correct answer is **choice B**, *will go*.

For **Example 2**, you must choose the verb that agrees with the subject. The subject in the sentence is *lions*. It is a plural noun, so it needs a plural verb. Only **choice D** contains a plural verb, *like*. **Choice D** is correct.

Example 3 asks you to identify which word is a **verb**. Verbs show action or being. The word that shows action in the sentence is *rose*, or **choice C**.

◎ Try It On Your Own

4 Next week, Rosa _____ a birthday cake for me.

 A makes
 B made
 C will make
 D made

5 Tim and Emmanuel ___ birthdays on the same day.

 A has
 B have
 C will have
 D having

6 Yesterday, I _____ my lucky pencil.

   A lost

   B losted

   C have lost

   D will lost

7 Mr. Garza _____ eight miles a day to stay in shape.

   A runned

   B run

   C runs

   D running

8 Which word in the sentence is a verb?

   The <u>telephone</u> <u>was</u> <u>one</u> of the <u>greatest</u> inventions.

   A telephone

   B was

   C one

   D greatest

9 Early telephones _____ displayed in museums.

   A is

   B are

   C be

   D am

10 We _____ on the phone yesterday.

   A speak

   B speaked

   C spoke

   D will speak

Test-Taking Tips

1 When completing a sentence with different word choices, say the sentence to yourself with each word choice. Choose the word that sounds right.

2 Watch for common mistakes. For example, "Mom drove Franco and I to school," is incorrect. You wouldn't say "Mom drove I to school." You would say "Mom drove me to school." Therefore, "Mom drove Fraco and me to school" is correct.

Go for it!

Unit Seven Practice Test

Estimated time: 15 minutes

Directions: Read each question and choose the best answer.

1 A pronoun—

   A takes the place of a noun.

   B shows action.

   C names a person, place, or thing.

   D shows being.

2 Which verb BEST completes the sentence?

Last night, we _____ dinner at 6 o'clock.

   A eat

   B will eat

   C eated

   D ate

3 Which phrase BEST completes the sentence?

_____ are the best swimmers on the team.

   A She and me

   B She and I

   C Her and me

   D Her and I

4 Which pronoun BEST completes the sentence?

Travis called _____ on the phone.

   A me

   B I

   C she

   D his

5 Which sentence is written correctly?

   A The birds is eating the crumbs.

   B The birds are eating the crumbs.

   C The birds eaten the crumbs.

   D The birds eats the crumbs.

GO ON

6 Which word BEST replaces the underlined words?

<u>The elephant</u> had a huge trunk.

A It

B We

C Him

D They

7 Which pronoun BEST completes the sentence?

The girls rode _____ bicycles to the park.

A them

B their

C they

D her

8 Which of the following underlined words is a noun?

<u>Although</u> <u>she</u> is shy, <u>Kathryn</u> <u>loves</u> to sing.

A Although

B she

C Kathryn

D loves

9 Which of the following nouns is formed correctly?

A foxs

B duckes

C washs

D wolves

10 Write a sentence using the word *freedom* as an abstract noun. (1 point)

_____

_____

_____

_____

STOP

Points Earned/Total = _____/10

Language
Lesson

17

Adjectives and Adverbs

Review the Standards (L.3.1.a, L.3.1.g)

- Explain the function of **adjectives** and **adverbs**
- Form and use **comparative** and **superlative** adjectives and adverbs

Q: What are **adjectives** and **adverbs**?

A: Study the chart below

Term	What it is	Examples
Adjectives	a word that describes a noun or pronoun	A small bird was singing in the tree. (*Small* describes *bird*.)
Adverb	a word that describes a verb or another adjective	The bird sang sweetly in the tree. (*Sweetly* describes *sang*.)

Q: How do I use **comparative** and superlative **adjectives** and adverbs?

A: Comparative and superlative are terms that have to do with adjectives and adverbs that compare two or more things.

Term	What it does	How it is formed	Examples
Comparative	compares two things	Add –er or *more*	She is **taller** than her sister. His time was **faster** than mine. Her hair is **more beautiful** than Tina's.
Superlative	compares three or more things	Add –est or *most*	She is the **tallest** in her family. He is the **fastest** player on the field. Of the three girls, her hair is the **most beautiful**.

Hint

Adverbs often end in –*ly*.

Never use both *more/most* and -*er*/-*est*.

GO ON

Try It

Directions: Answer the questions that follow.

1 What word is the adjective in the sentence?

Hans is the shortest of the three boys.

A Hans
B is
C shortest
D boys

2 What word is the adverb in the sentence?

Walk carefully across the frozen pond.

A Walk
B pond
C carefully
D frozen

3 Rewrite the following sentence so that the comparison is correct.

We soon realized that my horse was more gentler than LaKeesha's.

_____

_____

_____

_____

To answer **Example 1**, you must identify an **adjective**, or describing word. Choice A, *Hans*, is a noun and the subject of the sentence. Choice B, *is*, is the verb. Choice D, *boys*, is a noun. Choice C, *shortest*, describes the noun *Hans*. Words that describe nouns are adjectives. **Choice C is correct.**

For **Example 2**, you must think about which word is an **adverb**. Adverbs describe verbs and adjectives. *Walk* is a verb, and *pond* is a noun. *Frozen* is describing the pond, so it is an adjective. *Carefully* is describing how to *walk*, a verb. The correct answer is **choice C.**

For **Example 3**, you must identify what is wrong with the **comparison**. The phrase *more gentler* is incorrect. It should be *gentler*.

Corrected sentence: *We soon realized that my horse was gentler than LaKeesha's.*

4   Which of the following underlined words is NOT an adjective?

The <u>blue</u> car drove <u>slowly</u> around the <u>narrow</u>, <u>curvy</u> roads.

A blue
B slowly
C narrow
D curvy

5   Of all of our class, Shawna is the ____.

A shorter.
B shortest.
C more shorter.
D most shorter.

6   To me, the ocean is the _____ place to vacation.

A funest
B funer
C most fun
D most funest

7   Which is ____, the hippopotamus or the rhinoceros?

A heavy
B heavier
C more heavier
D heaviest

8   I think that science is the _____ subject in school.

A interestingest
B interestinger
C most interesting
D more interesting

9   Who moves _____, the turtle or the sloth?

A slower
B slowest
C more slower
D most slower

Language
Lesson
18

Conjunctions and Types of Sentences

Review the Standards (L.3.1.h, L.3.1.i, L.3.3.b)
- Use **coordinating** and **subordinating conjunctions**
- Produce **simple**, **compound**, and **complex** sentences
- Understand and use **standard English**

Q: What are **conjunctions,** and how do I use them?

A: Conjunctions are words that link groups of words together. The most common conjunctions are *and, but, or,* and *so*. These are **coordinating conjunctions**.

Examples: Shaina <u>and</u> Mitch are playing soccer.

My brother plays football, <u>but</u> I like baseball better.

Subordinating conjunctions are used to connect clauses in a sentence. Some of the most common ones are *after, who, before, because, if, since, when*, and *that*.

Example: <u>When</u> I finish my homework, I can play outside.

Emily is the one <u>who</u> finished first in the spelling bee.

Q: What are **simple**, **compound**, and **complex** sentences?

A: Study the table below.

Type of sentence	Definition	Examples
Simple	One subject or compound subject and one verb or compound verb	<u>Sue and I went swimming at the pool.</u> <u>We swam for an hour and went home.</u>
Compound	Two complete sentences joined by a conjunction	<u>Wang loves pizza, but Jimmy loves tacos.</u>
Complex	One complete sentence with one subordinate/ dependent clause	After I came home, <u>I walked my dog.</u>

Q: What is **standard English**, and when should I use it?

A: Standard English is the formal language used in schools, in newspapers, and on the radio. It uses the rules of grammar accepted by English speakers. Slang or words that are only used in certain parts of the country are not standard English. You should use standard English when you are writing for school or for other formal situations.

Try It

Directions: Answer the following questions.

1   Which of the following is a simple sentence?

  A Kathryn loves to sing.
  B Kathryn loves to sing, and she also loves to dance.
  C Even though she is shy, Kathryn loves to sing.
  D Even though she is shy, Kathryn loves to sing, and she also loves to dance.

2   Which of the following is a compound sentence?

  A Dad bought a car and loved it.
  B Dad loved the new car.
  C Dad loved the new car that we bought.
  D Dad bought a car, and we loved it.

3   Use a conjunction to combine the following sentences into a compound sentence.

  Gina is rarely early. She is never late.

  _____

  _____

  _____

4   Correct the following sentence so that it uses standard English.

  I ain't going to be late to school tomorrow.

  _____

  _____

  _____

  Examples 1 and **2** test your knowledge of different kinds of sentence structure.
Example 1 asks you to identify a **simple sentence**. A simple sentence has one subject and
one verb. All the answer choices have one subject, *Kathryn*, but choice A is the only one with
one verb, *sing*. **Choice A** is correct.

  Example 2 asks you to identify a **compound sentence**. A compound sentence is two
or more simple sentences joined together, usually by a comma and the word *and*. The only
answer choice that is a compound sentence is choice D, *Dad bought a car, and we loved it.*
Choice D is correct.

  For **Example 3**, you need to combine the sentences to create a compound sentence.
A compound sentence has two sentences combined with a **coordinating conjunction**
such as *and, but, for,* or *or*. The two sentences show contrasting ideas, so *but* is the best
conjunction to use.

  Correct: *Gina is rarely early, but she is never late.*

Example 4 asks you to think about the rules of standard English. *Ain't* should not be used in formal writing. Instead you should use *am not*.

Correct: *I am not going to be late to school tomorrow.*

◎ Try It On Your Own

5 What kind of sentence is this?

Sarah and my brother wore their new rain boots.

   A simple
   B compound
   C complex
   D none of the above

6 Choose the BEST combination of the following sentences.

I went to the movies. I bought a huge tub of popcorn.

   A I went to the movies, but I bought a huge tub of popcorn.
   B When I went to the movies, I bought a huge tub of popcorn.
   C I went to the movies I bought a huge tub of popcorn.
   D I went and bought a movie and a huge tub of popcorn.

7 The following sentences contain slang. Rewrite the passage so that it is written in standard English. (3 points)

Solar power is an awesome way to save energy. In fact, our school is installing solar panels this fall. How cool is that!

_____

_____

_____

_____

Test-Taking Tips

1 Watch out for answer choices that are not real words, such as *shorterer*.

2 For questions about standard English, remember that slang and other informal words and phrases are not standard English. Eliminate any choices with *ain't, y'all, cool,* and other types of slang.

Go for it!

Unit Eight Practice Test

Estimated time: 15 minutes

Directions: Read the following questions. Then choose the best answer.

1 Read the sentence and decide which word is a noun.

The small dog wore a light blue sweater.

A small
B dog
C light
D blue

2 Which of the following words is an adjective?

The happy squirrel jumped quickly from branch to branch.

A happy
B squirrel
C jumped
D quickly

3 Ahmad is a _____ runner than Jack.

A more faster
B faster
C most faster
D fastest

4 Which of the following is a compound sentence?

A I love snowy days.
B Jacob and I love snowy days.
C I love snowy days, but Jacob hates them.
D I love snowy days and Jacob.

5 Which of the following is a simple sentence?

A As long as I'm wearing socks, my feet are warm.
B My feet are warm.
C My feet are warm, and I'm not wearing shoes.
D My feet are warm, but my hands are cold.

GO ON

6 Combine the following sentences using the subordinating conjunction *although*. Be sure to use a comma. (2 points)

I am in third grade. I am taller than most sixth-graders.

_____

_____

7 Create a compound sentence from the following sentences. Use the correct punctuation. (2 points)

I love to watch movies. Jen would rather read a book.

_____

_____

8 Which of the following is written in standard English?

A I be going to my grandma's house this weekend.

B The school just spent $200,000 bucks on new playground equipment.

C It ain't cool for you to forget your homework again.

D The apples we ate for lunch were very sweet and crisp.

Points Earned/Total = _____/10

Language
Lesson
19

Capitalization

Review the Standard (L.3.2.a)
- **Capitalize** words in titles, holidays, proper nouns, and geographical names

Q: What words must be **capitalized**?

A: The chart below shows some of the rules of **capitalization**.

Capitalization Basics

☞ Capitalize "firsts": the first word in a sentence, in a title, in a quotation, and in the salutation and closing of a letter.

> My teacher said, "Your work is very good."
>
> The Children of the Night
>
> Dear Uncle Ed,
>
> Yours truly,

☞ Capitalize proper nouns, including the names of people and geographical places.

> Mrs. Tara J. Fenter
>
> 430 Lincoln Street
>
> Chicago, Illinois

☞ Capitalize the pronoun *I*, days, holidays, months, and adjectives formed from names of persons and places.

> My brother and I like to fish.
>
> Friday, February 8
>
> a Japanese drawing

☞ Capitalize the first, last, and any important words in titles of books, newspapers, and magazines. Do not capitalize *a*, *an*, or *the* unless it is the first word.

> The Evening News
>
> The Stinky Cheeseman
>
> Harry Potter and the Deathly Hallows

GO ON

Try It

Directions: Read the following questions. Then choose the best answer.

1   Which sentence uses capitalization correctly?

  A we took a tour at a famous garden.
  B The guide's name was mr. Roger.
  C He told Uncle Ray and me to stand in front.
  D At the end of the tour, i thanked the guide.

2   Rewrite the following sentences using correct capitalization.

  I can't wait until december. We are jewish, and our family celebrates hanukkah beginning monday, december 8.

  _____

  _____

  _____

3   Which of the following sentences contains the correct capitalization?

  A What did you do on the fourth of July?
  B We went to disneyland.
  C Tara, Manny, and i love to ride the rides.
  D Disneyland is in California.

  Example 1 asks you to identify correct **capitalization**. In choice A, *we* should be capitalized because the first word of a sentence is always capitalized. The word *mr.* in choice B should be capitalized because it is the man's title. *I* should be capitalized in choice D because it is a proper noun—the name of a specific person, place, or thing. Choice C is the only sentence that uses capitalization correctly. *Uncle Ray* is capitalized because it is a proper noun. **Choice C** is correct.

  Example 2 asks you to correct the capitalization errors in the sentences. Read the sentences carefully and underline any words that should be capitalized but aren't. Remember that holidays, proper nouns, days of the week, and months of the year are capitalized.

  Corrected sentences: *I can't wait until December. We are Jewish, and our family celebrates Hanukkah beginning Monday, December 8.*

  For **Example 3**, you must decide which of the answers contains correct capitalization. Read each choice carefully. When you see an error, cross out the choice. In choice A, *Fourth* is not capitalized. In choice B, *Disneyland* is a proper name and should be capitalized. The *i* in choice C is not capitalized. Thus, the correct answer is **Choice D**.

4   Which of the following titles is correctly punctuated?

    A *Judy moody predicts the Future.*
    B *Charlotte's web*
    C *Charlie And The Chocolate Factory*
    D *The Case of the Missing Key*

5   Which of the following is correctly capitalized?

    A a collie named lassie
    B a Movie starring mickey mouse
    C the composer Beethoven
    D the corner of fifth and Park Avenue

6   Which of the following is correctly capitalized?

    A Augusta, Maine
    B uncle Dwayne
    C russian tea
    D pine Lake

7   Which of the following sentences contains correct capitalization?

    A Please write to Ms. Jayne Walker in El Paso, Texas.
    B My Family is from the island of Samoa.
    C I love to eat chinese food with chopsticks.
    D The School is located on Main Street.

8   Rewrite the following sentences using correct capitalization. (4 points)

My birthday is august 9. My uncle jack told me he would take me to the Movies for my birthday.

_____

_____

_____

_____

Language
Lesson
20

Punctuation

Review the Standards (L.3.2.b, L.3.2.c, L.3.2.d)

- Use **commas** in addresses, items in a series, and compound sentences
- Use commas and **quotation marks** in dialogue
- Form and use possessives

Q: When should I use **commas**, apostrophes, and **quotation marks**?

A: The following chart will help you review **commas**, apostrophes, and **quotation marks**.

Commas

☞ Place commas in addresses when written in a sentence. Commas go between the street and the city, between a city and a state, and between the address and the rest of the sentence.

> She lives at 2535 Rodeo Drive, Denver, Colorado, during the summer.

☞ Put a comma before the conjunction (*and, but, or, for*) in a compound sentence.

> My brother is a swim champion, but I won't go near the water.

> I will come to the party later, or I may stay home.

☞ Use commas to separate words in a series.

> I need a needle, some thread, and a button.

☞ A comma is used when writing dialogue to set off the speaker's tag (*he said*) from the speaker's exact words.

> Ling said, "Please shut the door."

> "Tickets, please," said the driver.

Apostrophes

☞ Use an apostrophe in a contraction.

> I'll   they're   isn't

☞ An apostrophe is also used to show ownership or possession.

> Caroline's shoe   bears' cave   men's bathroom

Quotation marks

☞ Use quotation marks before and after a speaker's exact words.

> Larry said, "Can you help me lift this box?

Try It

Directions: Read the following questions. Then choose the best answer.

1 Which sentence is punctuated correctly?

   A Mom said, "Please walk the dog."

   B Mom said, "Please walk the dog.

   C "Mom said, Please walk the dog."

   D Mom said, Please walk the dog."

2 Which sentence is punctuated correctly?

   A I have tests today in math, reading, and music.

   B I have tests today in, math reading and music.

   C I have tests today in math reading and music.

   D I have tests today in math reading, and music.

3 Find two punctuation errors in the following sentences. Then rewrite the sentences correctly on the lines below.

   I wanted to go rock climbing but Jackson wanted to go skateboarding. Instead we went to Jacksons house and played video games.

   _____

   _____

   _____

   _____

   Example 1 asks you to find the answer choice that has correct **punctuation**. The phrase "Please walk the dog" is something someone said. It is a quotation. Quotations need to be surrounded by quotation marks. **Choice A** is correct.

   To answer **Example 2**, you need to understand how to use **commas** correctly. This sentence contains items in a series, which require the use of commas. **Choice A** is correct because it includes commas between each item in the series. All the other answer choices are missing commas or have commas in the wrong place.

   For **Example 3**, you must find two punctuation errors. The first sentence has two clauses joined by the conjunction *but*. This means that a comma must be used before the conjunction. In the second sentence, *Jacksons* needs an apostrophe to show ownership. It should be changed to *Jackson's house*.

   Correct: *I wanted to go rock climbing, but Jackson wanted to go skateboarding. Instead we went to Jackson's house and played video games.*

4 Which sentence is punctuated correctly?

    A Wev'e been waiting for you.

    B W'eve been waiting for you.

    C Weve been waiting for you.

    D We've been waiting for you.

5 Which of the following is correct?

    A My grandmother lives at 1279, Shoreline Court, Muskegon, Michigan.

    B My grandmother lives at 1279 Shoreline Court, Muskegon Michigan.

    C My grandmother lives at 1279 Shoreline Court Muskegon, Michigan.

    D My grandmother lives at 1279 Shoreline Court, Muskegon, Michigan.

6 Rewrite the following sentences so that they contain correct quotation marks and commas. (5 points)

Don't go in the water said Miquel.

The waves are too high added Sue.

_____

_____

_____

_____

Spelling

Review the Standards (L.3.2.e, L.3.2.f)

- Spell high-frequency words correctly
- Apply the rules for adding **suffixes** to base words
- Use spelling patterns and other strategies in writing words

Q: What spelling rules will help me become a better speller?

A: Here are a few hints to help you become a better speller.

☞ Memorize the spellings of words used frequently.

Examples: *their, there, a lot, our, because, again, finally, friend, really*

☞ Remember the rules for making plurals and adding endings.

When you write the plural of a word that ends in a consonant and then *y*, change the *y* to an *i* and add *-es*.

Examples: *city/cities, cry/cries*

If the word ends with a vowel, and then *y*, just add *s*.

Examples: *key/keys, monkey/monkeys*

☞ Remember the rules for adding endings.

When you add an ending (suffix) to a one-syllable word that ends with one vowel and one consonant, double the consonant before you add the ending.

Examples: *brag/bragged, big/bigger*

If the word ends with two consonants, just add the ending.

Examples: *hard/harder, rock/rocked*

If a word ends in *y*, change the *y* to *i* and add the ending.

Examples: *happy/happiness, beauty/beautiful*

☞ Remember key spelling patterns.

Here is a rhyme to help you remember when to use *ie* and *ei*.

Put I before E   (*believe, piece, thief*)

Except after C   (*ceiling, receive*)

Or when the sound is long *a*

As in *neighbor* and *weigh*.   (*eight*)

☞ In word families, words have some of the same combinations of letters and the same sound. Remember the words with the same patterns of letters.

Examples: *delight, light, sight*
bought, fought, thought

GO ON

Try It

Directions: Read the following questions. Choose the best answer.

1   Complete the sentence by choosing the correct spelling of the word.

Many small _____ live in the forest.

A aminals
B annimals
C animels
D animals

2   Which word in the sentence is NOT spelled correctly?

I live in the howse at the end of the street.

A live
B howse
C end
D street

3   Each sentence in the following paragraph contains one misspelled word. Cross out the misspelled words and write them correctly on the lines below.

I would like to have alot of animals. I asked my parents for five puppys. Thier answer was, "How about five guppies?"

_____

_____

Example 1 asks you to find the word that is spelled correctly. **Choice D**, *animals*, is correct.

Example 2 asks you to choose the word in a sentence that is spelled incorrectly. All the words in the sentence are spelled correctly except for *howse*. **Choice B** is correct.

Example 3 asks you to identify misspelled words in a paragraph. Read the paragraph carefully and cross out any misspelled words. The word *alot* is incorrect in the first sentence. In the second sentence, the word *puppys* is misspelled. The *y* should be an *i* with *-es* as the ending. In the last sentence, the word *Thier* is misspelled. The *i* comes after the *e*.

Corrected words: *a lot, puppies, Their*

4 Which of the following plural words is correct?

   A cherries

   B babys

   C familyes

   D dictionarys

5 All of the following words are spelled correctly EXCEPT—

   A because.

   B again.

   C finaly.

   D believe.

6 Each of the following sentences contains one spelling error. Cross out the misspelled words and write them correctly on the lines below. (5 points)

   A new nieghbor just moved in upstairs. He makes a lot of noise at nite. I have a tuff time going to sleep. I started playing my music realy loudly. Hopefully he will be queiter.

_____

_____

_____

Test-Taking Tips

1 Check each word in a sentence carefully for errors in spelling. If a word doesn't look right to you, look at it again. It might be a misspelled word.

2 If you see a group of words with more than one capital letter, pay close attention. The words might need all of the capital letters, but they might not.

3 Watch for missing or misplaced punctuation in sentences. Apostrophes in contractions and nouns of ownership are often left out in test questions. Missing or misplaced commas are easy to overlook, so always examine each punctuation mark carefully. A period where a question mark or exclamation point should be can be hard to see.

Go for it!

Unit Nine Practice Test

Estimated time: 15 minutes

Directions: Read the following questions. Then choose the best answer.

1   Complete the sentence by choosing the correct spelling of the word.

We ate _____ for breakfast.

   A tost
   B toste
   C toast
   D taost

2   Complete the sentence by choosing the correct spelling of the word.

My friend was _____ at me.

   A smileing
   B smilling
   C smilin
   D smiling

3   Which word in the sentence is NOT spelled correctly?

Please lissen to the pretty music.

   A Please
   B lissen
   C pretty
   D music

4   Which sentence uses capitalization correctly?
   A Arnetta johnson wrote this book.
   B she is a famous author.
   C She was born on a farm in Canada.
   D Her birthdate was march 4, 1970.

5   Which sentence uses capitalization correctly?
   A Last year we were in Mrs. Santos's class.
   B Our Room was bright and sunny.
   C This september we will get a new teacher.
   D I hope my friend ellie is still in my class.

Directions: Read the following paragraph and answer the questions that follow.

For New Year's, we went to a cabin in (6) <u>denver Colorado</u>. Our cabin was nice and cozy. Outside it was (7) <u>raining sleeting and snowing</u>. We read the last chapter of the book (8) <u>*the Best Christmas pageant Ever*</u>. We will be home on January 6.

6 Which of the following is correct?

   A Denver, Colorado

   B denver, Colorado

   C Denver Colorado

   D denver, colorado

7 Which of the following is correct?

   A raining sleeting, and snowing

   B raining sleeting and, snowing

   C raining, sleeting, and snowing

   D raining, sleeting, and, snowing

8 Which of the following is correct?

   A *The Best Christmas pageant Ever*

   B *The Best Christmas Pageant Ever*

   C *the best Christmas pageant ever*

   D *The best christmas pageant Ever*

9 Which of the following is correct?

   A 1301 NW Shoreline Court, Ankeny, Iowa

   B 1301, NW Shoreline Court, Ankeny, Iowa

   C 1301, NW Shoreline Court, Ankeny Iowa

   D 1301 NW Shoreline Court, Ankeny Iowa

10 Which of the following sentences is correctly punctuated?

   A I wanted to go out for pizza but we ordered Chinese food instead.

   B I love to eat fortune cookies and my mom loves crab rangoon.

   C Her fortune cookie read, "All your hard work will soon pay off."

   D My mom said That's good to know.

Points Earned/Total = _____/10

Language Lesson 22

Word Parts

Review the Standards (L.3.4.b, L.3.4.c)

- Use **prefixes**, **suffixes**, and **roots** to decode and define words

Q: How can **affixes** and **root** words help me understand the meanings of new words?

A: Many words can be broken down into word parts. These parts include **affixes** (**prefixes** and **suffixes**) and **roots**. When you know the meanings of commonly used word parts, it can help you read and understand the meanings of new words. Study the chart below.

Prefixes	Meanings	Examples
dis-	opposite of	**dis**honest, **dis**like
mis-	wrongly	**mis**behave, **mis**label
un-	not	**un**happy, **un**done

Suffixes	Meanings	Examples
-less	without	harm**less**, blame**less**
-ly	in a way that is	quick**ly**, slow**ly**
-ness	state of being	sad**ness**, well**ness**

Affix/Root	Meaning	Examples
graph	write, draw	autograph, biography
ped	foot	biped, pedal
tele	far away	television, telephone
therm	heat	thermal, thermostat

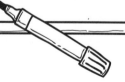

Directions: Read the selection. Then answer the questions that follow.

Dancing Bees

Did you know that honeybees dance? No, they don't wear little tiny tap shoes on their feet. They dance to talk with other bees and tell them where to find pollen, or the dust from flowers, for making honey.

Bees not only take care of themselves, but they help people too. Bees are <u>unusual</u> because they are the only insects that make food for humans. They also help plants to grow and bloom each year by spreading pollen.

Honeybees live together in a group called a *colony*. Each colony contains thousands of bees. Most of them are a type called *workers*. These tiny bees do all the work in the hive, or bee home. They fly out of the hive to gather food and water. They bring pollen and nectar, or flower juice, from plants back to the hive. They will store it for food during the winter. Workers fly around outside the hive searching for flowers.

If a worker finds flowers, it <u>quickly</u> flies back to the hive to tell the others. It tells them which way to go by dancing. For example, the returning bee might dance in circles. That means that the flowers are nearby. If the flowers are far from the hive, the <u>worker</u> dances in the direction it wants the other workers to go.

If a honeybee ever buzzes around you, don't swat at it. It just might be on its way to the hive to make the honey you like to eat.

GO ON ➡

1 Read this sentence from the selection.

Bees are <u>unusual</u> because they are the only insects that make food for humans.

In this sentence, <u>unusual</u> means—

A not usual.

B usual again.

C almost usual.

D very usual.

2 Read this sentence from the selection.

If a worker finds flowers, it <u>quickly</u> flies back to the hive to tell the others.

In this sentence, <u>quickly</u> means—

A able to be quick.

B not quick.

C in a quick way.

D the state of being quick.

3 Read this sentence from the selection.

If the flowers are far from the hive, the <u>worker</u> dances in the direction it wants the other workers to go.

What is the root word of <u>worker</u>?

A wor

B work

C or

D ork

Example 1 asks you about the meaning of the word *unusual*. To decide the meaning of a word, you can look at its parts, including the **prefix**. A prefix is the part of a word that comes before the **root**, or base, and changes its meaning. The prefix *un-* means "not." So *unusual* means "not usual," **choice A**.

Knowing the meaning of a **suffix** will help you answer **Example 2**. A suffix is a word ending that changes the meaning of the root. The suffix *-ly* means "like" or "in a certain way." It changes the meaning of the root *quick* to "in a quick way." The correct answer is **choice C**.

Example 3 asks you about a **root word**. A root word is the base part of the word, without any prefixes or suffixes. The root of *worker* is *work*, **choice B**.

Directions: Read the following passage and answer the questions that follow.

Beth and her mother were working. They were taking their cold weather clothes out and putting their hot weather clothes away. Beth carefully folded all her shorts and <u>sleeveless</u> shirts and carried them into the spare room. Her mother stored them in a chest drawer. She handed Beth the winter clothes to hang in her closet. The first piece was Beth's down vest. Beth loved that vest. As she skipped back to her room, Beth smiled to herself. She was <u>preparing</u> for her favorite season of the year—winter.

4   Reread this sentence from the passage.

Beth carefully folded all her shorts and <u>sleeveless</u> shirts and carried them into the spare room.

In this sentence, the word <u>sleeveless</u> means—

A with short sleeves.

B with no sleeves.

C with puffy sleeves.

D with long sleeves.

5   The prefix *pre-* as used in the word <u>preparing</u> means—

A after

B before

C new

D again

6   Read the following sentence.

Beth would be <u>unprepared</u> for any warm days in the fall.

The word *unprepared* means—

A not ready

B more than ready

C ready

D a little ready

Language Lesson 23

Word Use

Review the Standards (L.3.5.b, L.3.5.c)

- Identify **connections** between words and their use
- Distinguish **shades of meaning** among words

Q: How can I make **connections** for words I read in a book and my own writing and speaking?

A: When you learn a new word, try to use it when you are talking to your parents or writing a story for your teacher. This will help you become familiar with the word. Make a connection by thinking about where you've heard the word used before.

Q: What are **shades of meaning** in words?

A: You know that synonyms are words that mean ALMOST the same thing.

   Cold: freezing, chilly, icy, cool

The shades of the meaning of the words *freezing* and *icy* communicate greater cold than the words *chilly* and *cool*.

Study these synonyms for *think*. Which sentences mean you are SURE that it will rain?

- I **know** it will rain today. (I'm positive.)
- I **think** it will rain today. (I'm not so positive.)
- I **believe** it will rain today. (I'm not positive, but I suppose it will happen.)
- I **wonder** if it will rain today. (I don't really know.)

Be sure to use the word that means exactly what you want to communicate.

 Try It

Directions: Read the following passage, and then answer the questions that follow.

What Is Lightning?

1   Have you ever <u>shuffled</u> your feet across the carpet and then touched someone? Did you get a shock or see a spark of electricity? This electricity is caused by friction. Friction is what results when two surfaces rub against each other.

2   Thunderstorms create friction too. Billions of ice, sand, and dust particles float in the clouds. Wind <u>whips</u> them around so they crash into each other. As these particles

crash together, friction is created, just like when you shuffle your feet across the carpet. Friction causes electricity. Lightning is a gigantic spark of electricity.

3   Lightning is one of nature's most exciting events. A bolt of lightning can be many miles long. It can shine brighter than ten million lightbulbs. It may spark between two clouds. Or it may spark between a cloud and something on the ground.

www.photos.com

4   Lightning is very hot. The heat makes air particles <u>expand</u>, or get bigger. As the heated air expands, it bumps into the air around it. All these air particles bumping into each other make a lot of noise. That noise is known as thunder. If lightning is nearby, then its thunder sounds like a loud crack. If lightning is far away, then its thunder turns into a rumbling sound before it reaches you.

5   Light travels faster than sound. Because of this, you may see a flash of lightning before you hear its thunder. The more time that passes between the light and the sound, the farther the lightning is from you. If you see a flash and hear a boom at the same time, it means the lightning is very close.

---

1   Which word has nearly the same meaning as the word *whips* used in the following sentence?

Wind <u>whips</u> them around so they crash into each other.

A moves

B floats

C runs

D blasts

GO ON

2 Which of the following sentences uses the word *shuffle* in the same way it is used in paragraph 1?

    A I <u>shuffled</u> the cards and then dealt them out to the players.

    B My mom told me to stop <u>shuffling</u> my feet, or I'd wear out my shoes.

    C The teacher <u>shuffled</u> the papers on her desk to find mine.

    D So many things were <u>shuffling</u> around in my head that I couldn't concentrate.

Example 1 asks you to think about **shades of meaning** of the words. The word *whips* implies that the wind is blowing very hard and violently. The word that has the most similar meaning is **choice D**, *blasts*.

For **Example 2**, you must make a connection between how *shuffle* is used in the passage and how it is used in the answer choices. You understand that in the passage *shuffle* means "to slide your feet across the floor." Thus, the best answer is **choice B**.

◎ Try It On Your Own

3 Which of the following words means almost the same as the word *hot* in the following sentence?

Lightning is very <u>hot</u>.

    A *warm*

    B *steamy*

    C *superheated*

    D *reheated*

4 In paragraph 4, the word *expand* is used. Use the word *expand* correctly in a new sentence.

_____

_____

_____

_____

Test-Taking Tip

To find the meaning of a word with a prefix or suffix, think about the meaning of the prefix or suffix. Then add that meaning to the root word.

Go for it!

Unit Ten Practice Test   Estimated time: 15 minutes

Directions: Read the following passage. Then answer the questions that follow.

School Bus Friends

Abby couldn't believe it. The first day of school was here already. Abby liked to think that she was <u>unafraid</u>, but she felt fear slowly <u>creeping</u> up the back of her neck. She and her family had lived in their new home since June. Abby hadn't met anyone who was in her grade at school. Actually, Abby hadn't met anyone her age at all. No kids lived in her new neighborhood. On her old street, there was someone her age living in every house. They all went to school together, played soccer together, and did everything together. Then Abby's mom changed jobs. Abby and her family moved to another state. Now there was no one to play with.

Abby was most worried because she had to ride a bus to school. Before, all her friends rode in car pools. As Abby waited with her mom for the bus, she stood on one foot and then the other foot. Mom asked, "Abby, are you cold? You're moving around a lot." Abby just shook her head. Mom looked down to <u>recheck</u> her watch. Then, like a giant dragon running through the mist, the front end of the bus roared toward them. The headlights shone brightly, and the engine <u>growled</u>. The door flew open, and Abby began the climb up the steps. She felt like she was being swallowed by a dragon.

With a big gulp, Abby started walking down the aisle. She tried to make herself <u>invisible</u>. One seat contained only one girl. She looked about Abby's age. Abby caught her breath and asked in a tiny voice, "May I sit down?"

The girl stared at Abby with big brown eyes. "I don't care," she answered. Abby slid into the seat along with her backpack. Both girls stared straight ahead. <u>Finally</u> Abby asked, "What's your name?"

www.photos.com

"Alison," answered the girl. "And don't talk to me. I hate it here!"

"So do I," whispered Abby.

Alison turned to face her. "Why?"

"Because I'm new here. And I miss my friends. I'm lonely. I don't know anybody here. I've never been to this school. I've never been on a bus before. And I miss my FRIENDS." A tear ran down Abby's face. She could feel the <u>sadness</u> that had been inside her since she left her old home.

GO ON

"Me too," answered Alison. Both girls looked at each other for a moment.

"How old are you?" asked Abby.

"Eight."

"Grade?"

"Third."

"Me too."

Before the bus drove into the school lot, both girls were talking as if they were old friends. They talked about how they could have their parents meet. Maybe their new lives in new homes would not be so terrible after all.

1 As used in the selection, what does the word <u>unafraid</u> mean?

A afraid again

B not afraid

C not able to be afraid

D full of fear

2 What is the root word of <u>creeping</u>?

A ing

B cr

C ping

D creep

3 Using the meaning of the prefix *re-*, what does the word <u>recheck</u> mean?

A look at again

B wind again

C fasten again

D clean off

4 Which of the following words has nearly the same meaning as the word <u>growled</u> in the following sentence?

The headlights shone brightly, and the engine <u>growled</u>.

A purred

B roared

C sounded

D chugged

5 Which of the following would help you make a connection to the word *car pool*?

A talking about the car pool you ride in to school

B describing your mom's car

C writing about going swimming

D drawing a picture of a car

6 The prefix *in-* as used in the word <u>invisible</u> means—

A not   C again

B over   D off

7 The root *vis* as used in the word <u>invisible</u> means—

A foot

B eye

C see

D talk

8 Based upon the meaning of the word *lonely*, the word *loner* means someone who—

A stays away from people.

B is a good leader.

C talks too much.

D tries to get attention.

Points Earned/Total = _____ /8

Mastery Test: Part 1

Estimated time: 50 minutes

Directions: Read the following story, and then answer the questions that follow.

The Frog and the Antelope

1   Once upon a time, there were two villages. Antelope was the chief of one village. No one could beat him at running. Many had tried. All gave up. Antelope was the fastest runner of all.

2   Antelope also had a deep singing voice. He was proud of his deep voice. He liked to brag about it.

3   Frog was the chief of the other village. He could not run fast. But he was a fast thinker. The only problem in Frog's village was that the frogs wanted deep singing voices like the antelope had. Frog thought of a way he could fix the problem.

4   Frog hopped along the road that led to Antelope's village. He found Antelope's house and went inside. They sat together and shared a meal. Then Antelope began to brag about his running.

5   "I can run as fast as the wind. Nobody can beat me in a race."

6   "I like to race too," said Frog.

7   "But you are not as fast as I am!" Antelope laughed.

8   "That's true," said Frog. "But I am a fast thinker."

9   "Thinking won't help you win a race," said Antelope.

10   "Let's see about that," said Frog.

11   "What?" asked Antelope. "You want to race me?"

12   "Yes," said Frog. "Let's race tomorrow at sunrise. We'll hold the race on the road between our two villages."

13   "It's a deal," laughed Antelope. "What shall we bet?"

14   "The only thing I have of value is my clothes," said Frog. "You must admit they are magnificent. See what a beautiful green color they are! And in the hot summer sun they are always cool as a mountain stream. The frogs will give the antelope their clothing if I lose the race."

15   "All right," agreed Antelope. "Now what do we antelope have of value that I could bet . . ." thought Antelope to himself.

16   "You have deep singing voices," suggested Frog. "If you feel so sure that you will win the race, why not agree to give us your voices if you lose?"

17   "That's a fine idea," agreed Antelope. "You have a deal."

18   Frog hopped back to his village. On the way, he thought of a way he could beat Antelope in a race. When he reached the village, he told the other frogs about his plan.

19   The next morning before sunrise, the frogs formed a long line between their village and the antelope village. They hid in the tall grass. Each frog was spaced one hop away from another frog. The chief frog was at the end of the line where the race would begin.

20   "All you frogs along the road, listen to me carefully," said the chief frog. "You are all in this race with me. When Antelope and I start this race, I will hop once down the road. Then the first frog hiding in the grass will hop forward once. The frog after him will then hop forward. The next frog will do the same. Be sure that each of you keeps one hop in front of Antelope. Since we are all wearing the same clothes, the Antelope will think you are all me."

GO ON

21   By now, the sun was out of bed and ready for the day. Antelope came out of his house. He walked confidently to the road to meet Frog. All the other antelope followed him to watch the race. They were all laughing at Frog.

22   "Are you ready?" asked Antelope.

23   "Yes, I am ready to win this race," replied Frog.

24   "Here we go," laughed Antelope, as he ran down the road. But Frog was always a little ahead of him. "Well, Frog is faster than I thought," said Antelope. "I had better run faster." So Antelope ran like the wind on a stormy day, but no matter how fast Antelope ran, Frog was always one hop ahead of him.

25   Out of breath, Antelope finally fell down before he reached the finish line. The last frog hiding in the bushes took one final hop and won the race.

26   The antelope watching the race were stunned. All the frogs started laughing. Antelope pulled himself up. He was huffing and puffing from running so fast. The last frog to cross the finish line was smiling and looking proud of himself.

27   "I can't believe that you are not out of breath like me," said Antelope. "I guess I misjudged you. Now I know that you are a faster runner than I am. You can all keep your clothes. And we will give you our deep singing voices."

28   "Ribbit!" croaked Frog, and smiled to himself.

---

1   What motivates Frog to challenge Antelope to a race?

   A He is tired of Antelope bragging.

   B He knows that he is faster than Antelope.

   C He wants the antelopes' deep singing voices.

   D He wants to get some exercise.

2   What lesson does this story teach?

   A Fast thinking is better than fast running.

   B It's okay to trick someone to get what you want.

   C Frogs are faster than antelopes.

   D Frogs are smarter than antelopes.

3   When Frog describes his clothes as "cool as a mountain stream," he is using what kind of figurative language?

   A metaphor

   B simile

   C personification

   D idiom

4   Study the sentence below.

   By now, the sun was out of bed and ready for the day.

   This means that—

   A it was morning and the sun was shining in the sky.

   B it was still night and the sun was not shining.

   C it was cloudy.

   D it was raining.

5   How is your point of view as a reader different from the point of view of Antelope?

   A We know that antelopes aren't fast runners.

   B We know that the frogs are tricking Antelope.

   C We know that frogs aren't really smart.

   D We know how the story will end.

Directions: Read the following poem, and then answer the questions that follow.

The Big Race

Hare and Tortoise met face to face
And settled on a time and place
For a very, very important race.

"I'm <u>fastest</u>, you'll see!" said Hare with glee.
5 "There's no way you will outrun me.
I'll beat you to the old oak tree!"

But Tortoise had not a single worry.
"I'll beat YOU if you don't <u>hurry</u>!
When the race begins, you better scurry!"

10 Moments later, the race began;
Tortoise crawled, and Hare ran.
"Win?" huffed Tortoise. "I know I can!"

Hare soon tired and slowed his pace
And napped, while Tortoise passed that place.
15 Slow and steady won that race!

6 Read this sentence from the poem.

I'll beat YOU if you don't <u>hurry</u>!

Which word means the same as <u>hurry</u>?

A try

B rush

C dance

D start

7 This passage is mostly about—

A an argument between Hare and Tortoise.

B a nap that Hare took.

C a race between Hare and Tortoise.

D the single worry that Tortoise has.

8 Which stanza explains the lesson of the story?

A stanza 1

B stanza 3

C stanza 4

D stanza 5

9 Retell the poem "The Big Race." Be sure to use complete sentences. (3 points)

_____

_____

_____

_____

_____

10 How does the illustration help you understand the setting and the characters in the story? (3 points)

_____

_____

_____

_____

_____

Directions: Use both "The Frog and the Antelope" and "The Big Race" to answer the following questions.

11 Study this diagram about two characters in the stories.

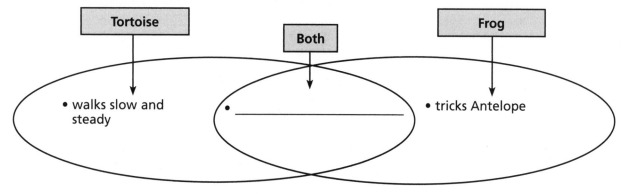

Which detail belongs in the center of the diagram?

A loses the race

B wins the race

C laughs at the loser

D wins a prize

12 One of the ways the two selections are alike is that—

A the winner of the race tricks the loser.

B the faster runner wins the race.

C the slower runner wins the race.

D no one wins the race.

13 Explain three ways the "The Big Race" and "The Frog and the Antelope" are different. Think about the form of the story; the characters; and the lesson, or moral, of the story. Use examples from BOTH selections to support your answer. (5 points)

_____

_____

_____

_____

_____

_____

_____

Directions: Read the following passage. Then answer the questions that follow.

This passage is part of a book about a teacher who is secretly teaching a freed slave how to read and write. When the mayor finds out, he is not happy.

Free to Learn

The mayor stopped. He took a deep breath. "I fear you wish to trick the town. Townsfolk see that new black man at your school each day."

Mrs. Blackwell tried to pretend. She scratched her head.

"Who?" she asked. "Oh. You mean the food peddler. He is just a farmer. He says his name is Freeman. From the edge of town. Fine carrots. Let me go get some for you to try."

The mayor shouted, "Come back, Mrs. Blackwell!"

Mrs. Blackwell stopped. "Yes?"

Tapping his foot, the mayor growled. "There is a law against teaching slaves to read and write. Beware."

She shook her head. "Teaching?"

The mayor stomped his foot. "Do not play games with me! I think you sneak the farmer into school. I think you are teaching him!"

Mrs. Blackwell's smile disappeared. She stared into the mayor's eyes.

"I do not teach the law, sir," she began. "But someone should teach law to you.

Benjamin Freeman is a freed slave. He is the property of no one. How will I break that law if I teach him?"

Anger bubbled from the mayor. His voice grew lower but louder.

"I will not see this village host a Negro Dame School. Words have power!" he said. "When you teach Negroes to read and write, you <u>arm</u> them with a powerful weapon."

A weapon, Mrs. Blackwell thought. She saw the pointer on her chair. If a student were as rude as the mayor, she would . . .

Mrs. Blackwell smiled at the idea. Then she quickly turned back to the mayor.

"Anyone who learns has a tool," she said. "Mayor, reading and writing are like a shovel and an ax. They are tools to help a person make more and do more. To *be* more."

The mayor threw up his hands. He did not give up, however.

He turned at the door. "I have warned you, Mrs. Blackwell. It would be a shame if you couldn't earn money to care for your children. The village would have to find a good home for them."

The mayor opened the door and stomped away.

14 Read the sentence below.

"When you teach Negroes to read and write, you <u>arm</u> them with a powerful weapon."

From the context, the word *arm* means—

A a part of the body between the shoulder and the wrist.

B to give something that helps.

C the ability to throw or pitch a ball.

D the sleeve of a shirt.

15 In the word *farmer* the root word is—

    A *arm.*

    B *er.*

    C *farm.*

    D *far.*

16 In the word *peddler*, the suffix *-er* means—

    A more or greater.

    B one who does something.

    C the opposite of.

    D under.

17 Why is the mayor visiting Mrs. Blackwell?

    A He wants to see how school is going.

    B He is thanking her for her work as a teacher.

    C He thinks she is teaching a black man at her school.

    D He wants to buy some food from a farmer.

18 How does Mrs. Blackwell feel as the mayor talks to her? Use details from the story to support your answer. (3 points)

_____

_____

_____

_____

_____

19 Mrs. Blackwell's actions in the story support the main idea that—

    A it takes courage to stand up for what you believe.

    B friends can be frustrating.

    C it's bad to keep a secret.

    D learning is only for some people.

Take a break. Then go on to Part 2.

GO ON

Directions: Read the following passage. Then answer the questions that follow.

You Are What You Drink

What do you reach for when you are really thirsty? Many kids first go for a soft drink, or soda. In fact, 56 percent of 8-year-olds in America drink soda daily. And one-third of teenage boys drink at least three cans of soda each day! But what are you really putting into your body when you chug a cola? Soft drinks are unhealthy. This is because of what they *contain* and what they *replace* in your diet.

Soft drinks contain large amounts of sugar. One can or bottle of soda contains all the sugar you need in a day. And you haven't even eaten anything! Think about everything else you eat each day. Do you see where your sugar intake may climb to unhealthy levels? Too much sugar can cause tooth decay. This can lead to **cavities**. Too much sugar can also cause you to gain too much weight.

Many soft drinks also contain **caffeine**. It is a natural drug found in tea leaves, coffee beans, cocoa (used to make chocolate), and cola nuts (used to give some soft drinks their flavor). It makes you feel more awake and alert. But it can also make your heart rate go up.

Caffeine can make you **dehydrated**. This means that your body gets weak because it doesn't have enough water. So on hot days or after you've exercised hard, it's more important to choose a drink without caffeine. Have you tried to talk to your mom, dad, or teacher before his or her first cup of morning coffee? This is not always pleasant. That's because caffeine can also be **addictive**. If you drink beverages with caffeine on a regular basis, your body will think it *needs* the caffeine for you to feel normal. Going without the caffeine can cause headaches and grumpiness. Depending on the level of addiction, after a few days or weeks of going without caffeine, these withdrawal symptoms go away. Your body goes back to feeling normal without the drug.

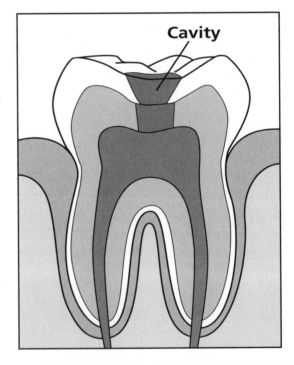

20 What is the main idea of this passage?

  A Soft drink companies spend millions each year on advertising.

  B Teenage boys are very thirsty.

  C Soft drinks are unhealthy.

  D Milk is a very healthy drink.

21 What would be a good question to ask while reading this passage?

   A When was the first soft drink company established?

   B How do soft drinks affect the body?

   C What is the best way to deal with a grumpy parent?

   D Which brand of coffee tastes the best?

22 Read the glossary.

Glossary

addictive	habit-forming
caffeine	a natural drug that can speed up one's heart rate or increase one's energy for a short time
cavity	a pit or hole in a tooth
dehydrated	not having enough water

Someone who is dehydrated should—

   A drink soda.

   B drink coffee.

   C eat chocolate.

   D drink water.

23 The illustration helps you understand—

   A where a cavity forms.

   B what each part of the tooth is called.

   C what causes cavities.

   D what a healthy tooth looks like.

24 Some words are in dark print because—

   A they are important new words to learn.

   B they are explained by the illustration.

   C they can't be looked up in a dictionary.

   D they are the chapter titles.

25 Study the following diagram.

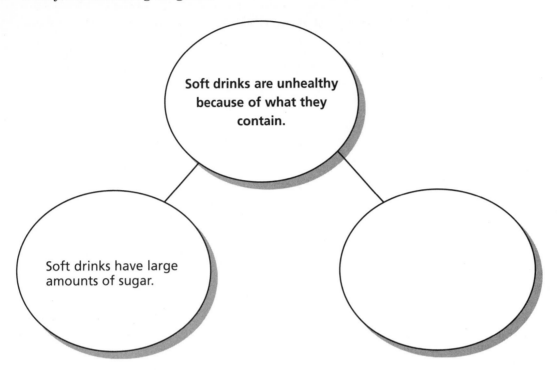

Which of the following important supporting details fits in the empty circle above?

A Too much sugar can cause tooth decay.

B Caffeine is found in tea leaves, coffee beans, cocoa, and cola nuts.

C One-third of teenage boys drink at least three cans of soda a day.

D Many soft drinks also contain caffeine.

26 Do you agree with the writer's point of view on soft drinks? Write a paragraph explaining whether you agree or disagree with the writer. Be sure to explain your own point of view. (3 points)

_____

_____

_____

_____

_____

_____

_____

_____

_____

Directions: Read the selection. Then answer the questions that follow.

The Revolutionary War (1776–1783) was a conflict between the 13 British colonies in America and the British government. Colonists wanted the freedom to set up their own government, and Britain wanted to keep control of the colonies.

Women of the Revolutionary War

1   During the late 1700s, many brave men fought to win the Revolutionary War. But did you know that American women were on the battlefield too?

2   Many women feared becoming poor when their husbands went off to war. In the 1700s, there were few ways for women to earn money. Some women had no choice but to follow their husbands to war.

3   These women made themselves very useful. They mostly sewed, washed, and cooked for the soldiers. They also cared for the wounded. As payment for this work, the army provided them with food.

4   But women also risked their lives on the battlefield. Soldiers could not fight the long, hot battles without water. Cannons also needed water to work properly. Women often were sent to search for nearby springs. They carried pitchers of the springwater to the battlefield, even during heavy fighting.

5   Some women worked beside their husbands at the cannons. This was a dangerous job as well. Firing cannons took the work of several people. Men always fired them. But women could help by getting the cannons ready.

6   One woman who helped at a cannon was especially brave. On November 16, 1776, the British attacked Fort Washington in New York. Margaret Corbin was there with her husband John. John's job was to help fire a cannon. Margaret helped him. When John was hit and fell to the ground, Margaret began firing the cannon herself. Her skill amazed the soldiers around her. She kept on firing until the battle was over.

7   Sadly, John died during that battle. Margaret lived, but she was badly injured. The injury left her with one useless arm.

8   The government later thanked Margaret for her service. She was the first American woman to receive money from the government to help her as she grew old.

9   Now, many history books tell about Margaret Corbin's brave actions. And in New York City, a plaque honors her. It describes her as "the first American woman to take a soldier's part" in the Revolutionary War.

27 Paragraph 2 explains—

A why women went to war.

B who went to war.

C what women did in the war.

D where women died in the war.

28 Which of the following sentences introduces a different way women helped in the Revolutionary War?

    A *But women also risked their lives on the battlefield.*

    B *These women made themselves useful.*

    C *They mostly sewed, washed, and cooked for the soldiers.*

    D *They also cared for the wounded.*

29 Which of the following details from the passage explains how Margaret Corbin was recognized for her bravery after the Revolutionary War?

    A *As payment for this work, the army provided them with food.*

    B *Her skill amazed the soldiers around her.*

    C *The injury left her with one useless arm.*

    D *And in New York City, a plaque honors her.*

Directions: Read the following passage. Then answer the questions that follow.

Molly Pitcher

1   Mary Ludwig Hays was born in 1744 near Trenton, New Jersey. At the age of thirteen Mary, who was known as Molly, was <u>employed</u> as a servant in Pennsylvania. When she was twenty-five years old, Molly married William Hays, a barber. When William went off to fight the British, Molly went with him.

2   In June 1778, William and Molly found themselves in the middle of the battle of Monmouth. William was in charge of firing one of the cannons. The day was sweltering and the soldiers were thirsty. They also needed water to cool down the hot barrel of the cannon and clean out the cannon between firings. Molly grabbed a bucket, or pitcher, and ran to a nearby spring to fill it. Whenever the men needed water, they would call out, "Molly, pitcher!" Molly would hurry over to them and give them a drink. In fact, during the Revolutionary War, "Molly Pitcher" became the nickname for all women who aided thirsty soldiers by bringing them water.

3   During the battle, she saw her husband fall down wounded. There were no other men to take her husband's place, so Molly asked the commanding officer if she could fire the cannon. Her request was granted, and Molly bravely "manned" the cannon. <u>According to legend</u>, at one point during the battle a cannonball flew between her legs and ripped off part of her skirt, but Molly only replied, "Well, that could've been worse." Molly fired the cannon until the British retreated from the battle.

4   After the battle, General George Washington asked about the woman he had seen loading a cannon. As a commemoration for her courage, General Washington made her an unofficial officer in the Continental Army. She was known from then on as "Sergeant Molly."

30 The major ideas in the text are written—

A in chronological order, or sequence of events.

B as causes and effects.

C in order of importance.

D in comparison and contrast.

31 Study the following sentence.

According to legend, at one point during the battle a cannonball flew between her legs and ripped off part of her skirt, but Molly only replied, "Well, that could've been worse."

The underlined phrase means that—

A none of the facts about Molly Pitcher are known to be true.

B the entire passage is an American legend.

C the story of the cannonball may or may not be true.

D the entire passage is fiction.

32 According to the context, the word *commemoration* means

A a way to remember.

B a payment.

C a punishment.

D a tax.

33 Study the following sentence.

At the age of thirteen Mary, who was known as Molly, was employed as a servant in Pennsylvania.

In which of the following sentences would the word employed be used in the same way it is used in the passage?

A I _____ my dog when I gave it a bath.

B My mother is _____ as a teacher at my school.

C We _____ our teacher to not give us a spelling test.

D The fireworks _____ when we lit them.

GO ON

Directions: Use both "Women of the Revolutionary War" and "Molly Pitcher" to answer the following questions.

34   Margaret and Molly are similar in all of the following ways EXCEPT—

   A they both supplied the soldiers with water.

   B they both fired cannons during a battle.

   C they both were hurt in battle.

   D they both were recognized and thanked for their service.

35   The fact that is ONLY found in "Women of the Revolutionary War" is—

   A water was needed for the cannons.

   B water came from nearby springs and rivers.

   C women went with their husbands to war.

   D women sewed, cooked, and did laundry for the soldiers.

> **Take a break. Then go on to Part 3.**

Directions: Answer the following questions.

36 The underlined word in the sentence is a(n)—

I <u>was</u> happy to see my grandma.

A adjective
B adverb
C pronoun
D verb

37 Which verb correctly completes the sentence?

The doctor looked at the X-ray of Ashad's leg and told him it was _____.

A break
B broken
C broke
D breaked

38 Which word in the sentence is an adjective?

<u>After</u> the baseball <u>game</u>, Vince's <u>white</u> shirt was covered in <u>dirt</u>.

A After
B white
C game
D dirt

39 Which of the following is a compound sentence?

A Cassie and Aaron are great at math and science.
B Cassie is great at math, and Aaron is great at science.
C Cassie is better than Aaron at math.
D Cassie is great at math and Aaron at science.

40 Which pronoun BEST replaces the underlined words?

<u>The students</u> are going on a field trip today.

A Them
B Us
C They
D He

41 Which pronoun BEST completes the sentence?

Eric and Donny moved _____ desks close together.

A his

B them

C its

D their

42 Complete the sentence by choosing the correct spelling of the word.

Our principal arrived _____.

A early

B erly

C earley

D erley

43 Which sentence uses punctuation correctly?

A There is a thorn in the lions' paw.

B There is a thorn in the lions paw.

C There is a thorn in the lion's paw.

D There is a thorn in the lion's' paw.

44 Complete the sentence with the word that is spelled correctly.

I borrowed a _____ from Marta.

A doler

B doller

C dallor

D dollar

45 Which sentence uses punctuation correctly?

A Give Chang paper, a pencil, and a book.

B Give Chang paper a pencil, and a book.

C Give Chang paper a pencil and a book.

D Give Chang paper a pencil and, a book.

46 What is the plural noun in the sentence below?

Rick loves to travel on airplanes.

A Rick

B loves

C travel

D airplanes

47 Which of the following uses commas and quotation marks correctly?

    A "Come here" I said to the dog.

    B Come here, I said to the dog.

    C "Come here, I said to the dog."

    D "Come here," I said to the dog.

48 Which of the following sentences uses correct capitalization?

    A My uncle is a Police Officer in my city.

    B We live in Atlanta, Georgia.

    C He has to work on Christmas and new year's eve.

    D His hobby is making traditional african food.

49 Which of the following BEST completes the sentence?

Cammie threw the ball _____ than Dwayne.

    A farthest

    B more far

    C farther

    D most far

50 Which of the following plural nouns is formed correctly?

    A meese

    B geese

    C dresss

    D churchs

51 Combine the following sentences into a complex sentence using a conjunction (*and, but, for*) and a subordinating conjunction (*when, although, because*). Be sure to use correct punctuation. (3 points)

My family went to the amusement park last Saturday. It rained the entire day. We still had a good time.

_____

_____

_____

_____

_____

_____

52 Which verb BEST completes the sentence?

The girls _____ to eat fresh vegetables.

A loves

B love

C loving

D be loving

53 Which of the following is an abstract noun?

<u>Martin Luther King Jr.</u> fought for greater <u>freedom</u> for <u>African</u> <u>Americans</u> in the <u>United States</u>.

A Martin Luther King Jr.

B freedom

C African Americans

D United States

Points Earned/Total = _____/67

Common Core
Grade
3

Keeping Score

	Points Earned / Total Points	Percent Score
Tryout Test	/67	%
Unit One Practice Test Reading Literature: Key Ideas and Details	/8	%
Unit Two Practice Test Reading Literature: Craft and Structure	/7	%
Unit Three Practice Test Reading Literature: Integration of Knowledge and Ideas	/7	%
Unit Four Practice Test Reading Informational Text: Key Ideas and Details	/6	%
Unit Five Practice Test Reading Informational Text: Craft and Structure	/12	%
Unit Six Practice Test Reading Informational Text: Integration of Knowledge and Ideas	/12	%
Unit Seven Practice Test Language: Nouns, Pronouns, and Verbs	/10	%
Unit Eight Practice Test Language: Adjectives, Adverbs, and Conjunctions	/10	%
Unit Nine Practice Test Language: Capitalization, Punctuation, and Spelling	/10	%
Unit Ten Practice Test Language: Vocabulary	/8	%
Mastery Test	/67	%

1. Fill in the number of points you earned in the Points Earned box.

2. Use the Finding Percent chart on page 154 to figure out your Percent Score. Then fill in the % box.

3. Compare your Percent Scores for the Tryout Test and the Mastery Test. See how much you've learned!

Finding Percent

→ Number of Points on Test

6

1	2	3	4	5	6
17%	33%	50%	67%	83%	100%

7

1	2	3	4	5	6	7
14%	29%	43%	57%	71%	86%	100%

8

1	2	3	4	5	6	7	8
13%	25%	38%	50%	63%	75%	88%	100%

10

1	2	3	4	5	6	7	8	9	10
11%	22%	33%	40%	50%	60%	70%	80%	90%	100%

12

1	2	3	4	5	6	7	8	9	10	11	12
8%	17%	25%	33%	42%	50%	58%	67%	75%	83%	92%	100%

67

1	2	3	4	5	6	7	8	9	10	11	12	13	14	15	16	17
1%	3%	4%	6%	7%	9%	10%	12%	13%	15%	16%	18%	19%	21%	22%	24%	25%

18	19	20	21	22	23	24	25	26	27	28	29	30	31	32	33	34
27%	28%	30%	31%	33%	34%	36%	37%	39%	40%	42%	43%	45%	46%	48%	49%	51%

35	36	37	38	39	40	41	42	43	44	45	46	47	48	49	50	51
52%	54%	55%	57%	58%	60%	61%	63%	64%	66%	67%	69%	70%	72%	73%	75%	76%

52	53	54	55	56	57	58	59	60	61	62	63	64	65	66	67
78%	79%	81%	82%	84%	85%	87%	88%	90%	91%	93%	94%	96%	97%	99%	100%

WRITING TEST WORKSHOPS

Writing Test Workshops

To the Student

Why Do I Need This Book?

This book will help you practice taking writing tests. You will learn how to—

- read a writing prompt
- get your ideas down on paper
- write to tell a story
- write to explain
- write about an opinion

How Will My Writing Be Scored?

Your writing test will be scored by test readers who use rubrics, or scoring guides. The rubric below lists 6 qualities of good writing. Read through each characteristic so you know how your writing will be graded.

Rubric Score: *1* is the lowest; *5* is the highest					
Ideas/Content—focuses on one main idea; the details add to the main idea	①	②	③	④	⑤
Organization—has a clear beginning, middle, and end; the order is easy to follow	①	②	③	④	⑤
Voice—communicates feelings and personality; the writing is unique	①	②	③	④	⑤
Word Choice—uses colorful, fresh words in the right places	①	②	③	④	⑤
Sentence Fluency—uses both long and short sentences that flow smoothly	①	②	③	④	⑤
Conventions—few or no spelling, capitalization, and punctuation errors	①	②	③	④	⑤

How to Manage Your Time During an Essay Test

You may have 20 to 45 minutes to complete a writing test, so it's important to have a plan.

If you have 20 minutes

◎ read the prompt, circle key ideas, brainstorm, and organize ideas (5 minutes)

◎ write the essay (10 minutes)

◎ edit and proofread (5 minutes)

How to Read a Prompt

A *prompt* is the assignment for a writing test. The prompt gives you directions. It also tells you what to write about.

◎ **Step 1**

Read through the entire prompt. Decide what the topic is.

◎ **Step 2**

Read through the prompt a second time, underlining key words (*explain, compare, tell*) that will help you focus your writing.

◎ **Step 3**

Look for key words or phrases you might use in your main idea statement.

Chen's Prompt

Here is a prompt for Chen's test. Look at the key words he underlined. They helped Chen understand exactly what he was supposed to do.

Prompt

Tell a story about a time when you had a special experience with an animal. The animal might be your pet or someone else's pet. Or it might even be a wild animal such as a squirrel or bird. Be sure to tell why this experience is one you remember.

Try It On Your Own

Now it's your turn. Read the prompt below. Then read it again. Underline the key words that would help someone taking a writing test.

Tell the story of a special day you remember. It might be a holiday, a birthday, or even the first day of school. Be sure to tell why this day is special to you.

GO ON ⇨

Narrative Writing Tests

Writing to Tell a Story

Review the Standards (W.3.3.a–d, W.3.4, W.3.5)

- Write **narratives** about real or imagined experiences
- Establish a **situation** and organize **events**
- Use **dialogue** and **descriptions**
- Use words and phrases to signal **event order**
- Provide an **ending**

When you write about something that happened to you, you are telling a story. This is also called writing a **narrative**. You might be asked to describe a true experience or to make up a story. Your story should have a beginning, a middle, and an ending.

Beginning

- introduces characters and a **situation**
- describes the setting (when and where the story takes place).
- may include a main idea statement:

  I'll never forget the first day of third grade.

Middle

- contains the main **events** of your story
- uses time order words: *next, then, later, when, after* to show **event order** (chronological order)
- includes the high point of your story
- uses **dialogue** and **description**

Description—precise, lively words

"The sky turned grey as I pedaled my bike toward my house."

Ending

- explains how everything turns out
- may tell what the experience taught you:

  I learned that you can't always count on things turning out the way you planned.

  or how an event changed you:

  Since I found that snake in our swimming pool, I always check before getting in!

"What's **dialogue**?" Joey asked.

"It's talking between characters," Mia replied.

Joey said with a laugh, "Oh, like what we're doing right now!"

Try It On Your Own

Putting your events in the order they happened will give your writing structure—a clear beginning, middle, and ending. Below are five events from a story. Number them from 1 to 5 in the order you think they happened. Which event is the high point of the story?

_____ My mom woke me up early on Saturday morning.

_____ I couldn't believe it when my mom said, "Pick out a kitten!"

_____ We drove to the pet store at the mall. In the window were lots of kittens.

_____ She told me we had a special errand to run.

_____ I named my kitten "Happy" because having her makes me the happiest person in the world!

Ted's Story

Below is a prompt Ted was given on a writing test. Help him out by underlining the key words. Then look at the prewriting story map he created below. Finally, read the story he wrote, which begins on the next page.

Prompt

Imagine that you are playing at the park with a friend. You're both tired, so you lean against a tree to rest. Suddenly the tree speaks to you. What does it say? Write a story about what happens next.

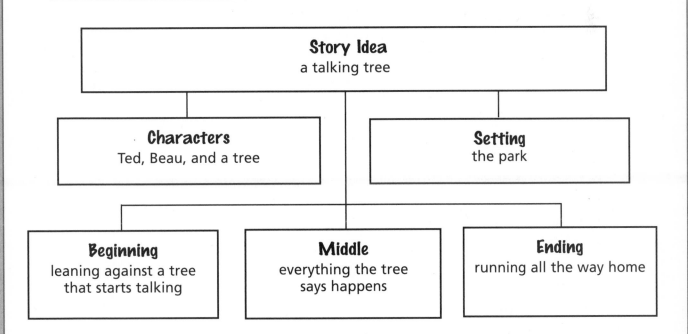

Story Idea
a talking tree

Characters
Ted, Beau, and a tree

Setting
the park

Beginning
leaning against a tree
that starts talking

Middle
everything the tree
says happens

Ending
running all the way home

GO ON

The Tree

One day Beau and I were playing at the park. After a while, we got tired, so we leaned against a tree. The tree was at least 50 feet tall with lots of green leeves that shaded us.

"Whew! I'm tired!" Beau said.

"Me, too!" I said.

Suddenly we heard the tree say, "Who gave you permission to lean on me?" He sounded kind of mad.

We had to think fast.

"That dandelion over there?" said Beau, pointing to his left.

"Very funny," said the tree.

As you can sea, this wasn't the most average thing in the world to happen. Beau was pretty freaked out. We didn't know what to say next, so we just standed there, staring up at the big tree.

Finally the tree said, "What? Cat got your tongue?"

Just then a big black cat and a scrawny orange cat jumps out of his leeves and grabbed our tongues. Now that was really over the top.

So now we were staring at the tree with two cats hanging off our tongues.

Suddenly the tree shouted, "I hear it's going to rain cats and dogs!"

So I said, "Don't be so loud." Or at least I tried to say that. But just then a gigantic Siamese cat fill on my head, and a big Saint Bernard fill on Beau's foot. At least Beau got licked. I got a scratch and a bite.

When we finally got the cats and dogs off our heads and tongues, I asked, "Does everything you say always happen."

"Of course," said the tree. "By the way . . ."

But we didn't wait to hear more. We ran all the way home without looking back. Beau and I deesided we'd never trust a tree again!

Looking at Ted's Writing

1. Underline the setting and characters of Ted's story.

2. Place a **B** in the margin next to the beginning.
   Place an **M** next to the middle.
   Place an **E** next to the ending.

3. Do the events in Ted's story seem to be in the order they happened?
   Yes _____ No _____

4. Put a **D** by dialogue and description.

5. Put a star by any words or phrases that show Ted's personality.

6. Correct mistakes in capitalization, punctuation, spelling, and grammar in Ted's writing.

Try It On Your Own

Now it's your turn to take a practice writing test. Follow the steps in order. If your teacher gives you a time limit, make a plan by filling in the amount of time you have to complete each step.

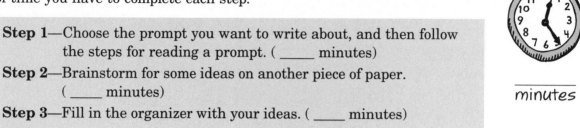

Step 1—Choose the prompt you want to write about, and then follow the steps for reading a prompt. (_____ minutes)

Step 2—Brainstorm for some ideas on another piece of paper. (_____ minutes)

Step 3—Fill in the organizer with your ideas. (_____ minutes)

Time Allowed

_____
minutes

Prompt ────────────────────

One day you're digging through some boxes on your closet shelf. You notice that one box has an opening in the side that looks like a small door. When you remove the lid, a voice inside yells, "Hey, put our roof back on!" Tell the story of what happens next.

Prompt ────────────────────

Things don't always go as planned. Tell the story of a time when you were disappointed because things didn't work out the way you thought they would.

────────────────────

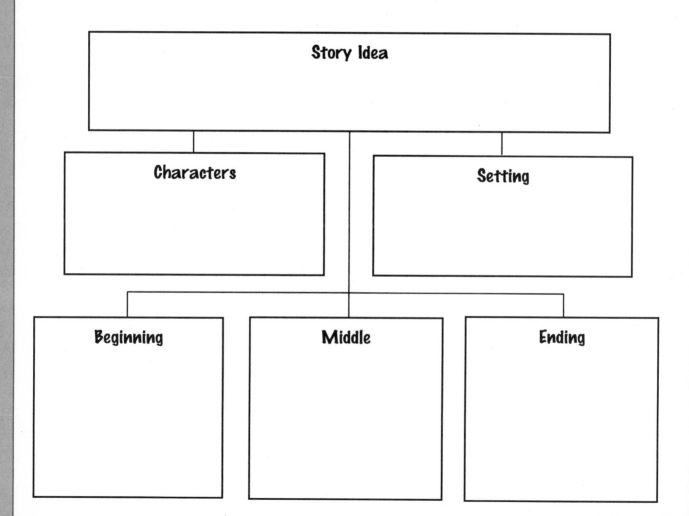

Story Idea

Characters

Setting

Beginning

Middle

Ending

Step 4—Using your story map as a guide, write your story on a separate piece of paper. (____ minutes)

Step 5—Go back and proofread your paper for mistakes in capitalization, puncutation, spelling, and grammar. (____ minutes)

How Did You Do?

Now evaluate your own writing (or ask a friend to evaluate your writing).

Consider This

1. **Ideas/Content** Underline the main idea.

2. **Organization** Is the story well structured? (yes or no)

   - Place a **B** in the margin next to the beginning, or introduction.

   - Place an **M** in the margin next to the middle.

   - Place an **E** in the margin next to the ending.

3. **Voice** Put a star by places where the personality of the writer shines.

4. **Word Choice** Circle three lively words in the story. If you can't find three lively words, look for places where they could be added.

5. **Sentence Fluency** Put a box around a section of the writing where both long and short sentences fit together smoothly. Write FLOW next to any sentences that seem too choppy.

6. **Conventions** Correct any mistakes you made in spelling or grammar.

Use your answers from the **Consider This** chart to help you fill in this rubric.

Rubric Score: *1* is the lowest; *5* is the highest					
Ideas/Content—focuses on one main idea; the details add to the main idea	①	②	③	④	⑤
Organization—has a clear beginning, middle, and end; the order is easy to follow	①	②	③	④	⑤
Voice—communicates feelings and personality; the writing is unique	①	②	③	④	⑤
Word Choice—uses colorful, fresh words in the right places	①	②	③	④	⑤
Sentence Fluency—uses both long and short sentences that flow smoothly	①	②	③	④	⑤
Conventions—few or no spelling, capitalization, and punctuation errors	①	②	③	④	⑤

Informative Writing Tests

Writing to Inform or Explain

Review the Standards (W.3.2.a–d, W.3.4, W.3.5)

- Write texts that inform or explain
- Introduce a topic and group related information together
- Develop the topic with **facts**, **definitions**, and **details**
- Use **linking words** and phrases to connect ideas
- Provide a **concluding statement** or section

When you write to **explain**, you provide information about a topic. The topic could be many things: why you like a particular book, how to take care of a pet, or the best way to make a friend.

Your writing-to-explain paper should also have a beginning, a middle, and an ending.

Beginning

In the first paragraph:
- grab your reader's attention
- include a topic sentence or main idea statement:

Here are some good ways to take care of a pet.

Grab Attention

- **Surprise your reader.** "One little brown bat can eat 600 mosquitoes in an hour!"

- **Entertain your reader.** Tell a story: "The first time I saw a bat, I screamed and hid in back of my big brother. I was sure it was going to land in my hair."

- **Challenge your reader.** Ask a question: "Are you one of the people who thinks bats are blind?"

Middle

- stick to the main idea by giving **facts,** explaining **details,** and giving **definitions**
- keep the flow going by using both long and short sentences
- use **linking words** such as *also, another, and, but*

The middle of your paper might explain:

how to feed and water a pet

how to bathe a pet

how to give a pet exercise

Ending

- review your supporting details:

So give your pet enough food and water, bathe it once a month, and make sure it gets plenty of exercise.

- provide a **concluding statement**:

Taking care of a pet is hard work, but it's worth it!

Try It On Your Own

The following is information from a writing-to-explain paper. The topic is "My family." Put a check mark next to the sentence that doesn't stick to the topic.

_____ My family includes my mom, my older brother Shawn, a cat, and two dogs.

_____ My family loves going to the movies.

_____ My mom works as a nurse at City General Hospital.

_____ I ride my bike to school every day.

_____ My brother and I like to play football together.

Kelsie's Paper

Below is a prompt Kelsie was given on a writing test. Help her out by underlining the key words for her.

Prompt

By this time, you've probably had several different teachers. Some of them you liked a lot. And some you might not have liked as well. Explain what you think makes a good teacher. Give examples of things that a good teacher does or doesn't do.

Before Kelsie began writing, she used an idea web to organize facts and details she wants to use in her paper.

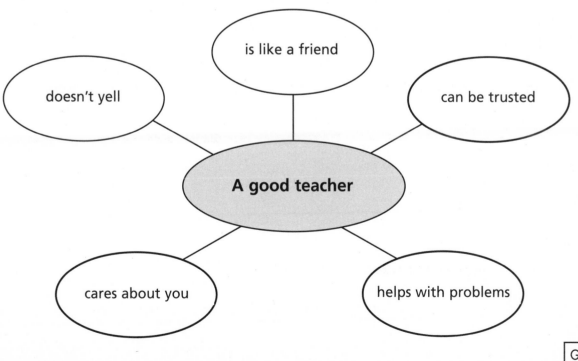

GO ON

A Good Teacher

There are many things that make a good teacher. I believe a good teacher is like a frend. When you first meat her, you don't think you're going to be very close? But then you start to get to no her better. A good teacher should be someone you can trust, someone who don't share things about you with other teachers or students. If you have a problem, you should be able to go to her, and she'll help you solve that problem. A good teacher should be someone who cares how you're doing in school. If you're not gitting good grades, she should give you idees to help you get your grades up. My brother gets terrable grades in school. He's in seventh grade. And a good teacher doesn't show anger at students. She doesn't yell at students and make them feal bad. Those are all the thinks that I think make a good teacher. When I have a good teacher, school is sow much fun!

Looking at Kelsie's Writing

1. Underline the main idea.
2. Place a **B** in the margin next to Kelsie's beginning.

   Place an **M** in the margin next to the middle of Kelsie's paper.

   Place an **E** in the margin next to the ending.
3. Put a line through any sentences that do not fit with Kelsie's main idea.
4. Where might Kelsie have used more exact nouns or lively verbs?
5. Correct mistakes in capitalization, punctuation, spelling, and grammar.

Try It On Your Own

Now it's your turn to take a practice writing test. Follow the steps in order. If your teacher gives you a time limit, make a plan by filling in the amount of time you have to complete each step.

_____ minutes

Step 1—Choose the prompt you want to write about, and then follow the steps for reading a prompt. (_____ minutes)

Step 2—Brainstorm for some ideas on another piece of paper. (_____ minutes)

Step 3—Fill in the organizer with your ideas. (_____ minutes)

Prompt _____

Classroom rules are important. Explain three important rules in your classroom. Be sure to explain why they are important. Describe which rule you believe is the most important.

Prompt _____

Do you have a hobby or something you really like to do? Explain what it is, how you do it, and why you like it.

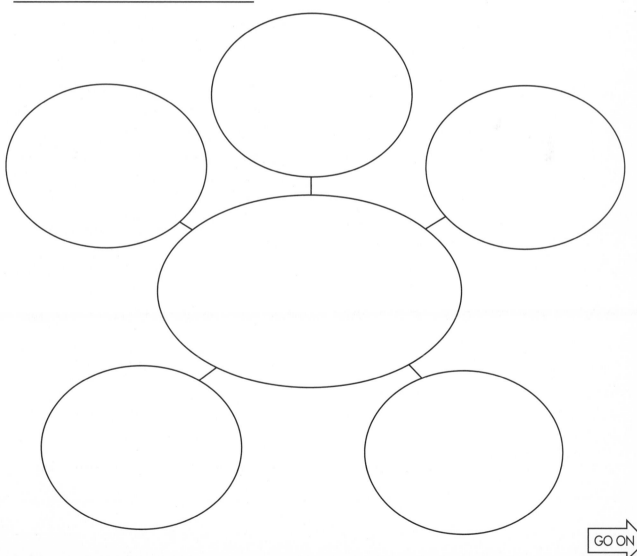

GO ON ➡

Step 4—Using your idea web as a guide, write your essay on a separate piece of paper. (_____ minutes)

Step 5—Go back and proofread your paper for mistakes in capitalization, punctuation, spelling, and grammar. (_____ minutes)

How Did You Do?

Now evaluate your own writing (or ask a friend to evaluate your writing).

Consider This

1. **Ideas/Content** Underline the main idea.
2. **Organization** Is the paper well structured? (yes or no)
   - Place a **B** in the margin next to the beginning, or introduction.
   - Place an **M** in the margin next to the middle.
   - Place an **E** in the margin next to the ending.
3. **Voice** Put a star by places where the writer's personality shines through.
4. **Word Choice** Circle three lively words in your the paper. If you can't find three lively words, look for places in your writing where you could insert them.
5. **Sentence Fluency** Put a box around a section of the writing where both long and short sentences fit together smoothly. Write FLOW next to any sentences that seem too choppy.
6. **Conventions** Put a check mark above any errors in spelling, capitalization, or punctuation.

Use your answers from the **Consider This** chart to help you fill in this rubric.

Rubric Score: *1* is the lowest; *5* is the highest					
Ideas/Content—focuses on one main idea; the details add to the main idea	①	②	③	④	⑤
Organization—has a clear beginning, middle, and end; the order is easy to follow	①	②	③	④	⑤
Voice—communicates feelings and personality; the writing is unique	①	②	③	④	⑤
Word Choice—uses colorful, fresh words in the right places	①	②	③	④	⑤
Sentence Fluency—uses both long and short sentences that flow smoothly	①	②	③	④	⑤
Conventions—few or no spelling, capitalization, and punctuation errors	①	②	③	④	⑤

I can improve my writing by _____

_____

Writing About an Opinion

MUNCH
MUNCH

Writing About an Opinion

Review the Standards (W.3.1.a–d, W.3.4, W.3.5)

- Write **opinion** pieces
- Introduce the topic, state an **opinion**, and list **reasons**
- Use **linking words and phrases**
- Provide a **concluding statement** or section

When you write to persuade, you are expected to state your opinion about a topic. This is called an *opinion statement*. Your opinion statement is the main idea of your paper. After you write your opinion statement, you try to convince your readers to agree with your opinion.

Beginning or Introduction

- get the reader's attention
- state your **opinion:**

  I think we should go to the zoo for our field trip.

Choosing the Best Reasons

To pick the best reasons, think about what your reader is concerned about. Which reason would persuade your parents to buy you a new bike?

- *It's not fair that I have an old bike and my sister has a new bike.*
- *If I had a new bike, I'd spend more time outside getting exercise and less time watching TV.*

Using Emotions

Sometimes writers try to convince the reader by making them feel sad, happy, angry, or guilty. Emotional appeals can be useful but should not take the place of good reasons.

All my friends have brand new bikes, but all I have is an old rusty one.

Middle

- give **reasons** that support your opinion:

  First, we'll learn about lots of interesting animals at the zoo.

  Another reason is that the zoo has a really fun gift shop.

  Finally, we'll get lots of fresh air and sunshine at the zoo.

- use **linking words and phrases** like *first, because, therefore, since, most importantly,* and *for example*

Ending or Conclusion

- restate your opinion statement
- end with a strong thought:

  This is why I think the zoo would be a great place to go on our class field trip. We'll all come back happy and healthy—and we'll know more about animals!

GO ON

Try It On Your Own

Practice writing your own opinion statement. Suppose you'd rather go to the art museum for the field trip. Write your opinion statement below.

_____

_____

_____

_____

_____

Now list three reasons that support your opinion.

1._____

_____

2._____

_____

3._____

_____

Then write a sentence or two to conclude your argument.

_____

_____

_____

_____

_____

_____

_____

Maya's Paper

Below is a prompt Maya was given on a writing test. Underline the key words for her. Then look over the list organizer she used to organize her thoughts. Finally, read her paper on the next page.

Prompt

What makes your town special? Does it have nice parks? Good schools? Friendly people? Write a paper to persuade people to move to your town.

Topic: Why my town is special

Opinion Statement: I think people should move to my town.

Reasons
1. My town has a water park.
2. There is a shopping mall.
3. It has nice neighborhoods.

Move to My Town

I think people should move to my town. My town has a brand-new water park. The park has a big blue water slide and a huge swimming pool. In the summer, the water feels so cool! My town also has a nice shopping mall. The mall has lots of different stores. And it has three restaurants and a place that sells big, gooey cinnamon rolls. When you walk through the mall you can smell the rolls. The neighborhoods in my town are nice to live in too. The people are friendly, and they keep their yards clean. They also have block parties in the summer. Those are fun because the kids all get to march in parades. So if you're moving, you should think about moving to my town. You'll love it here!

Looking at Maya's Writing

1. Place a **B** next to the beginning of the paper.
   Place an **M** next to the middle.
   Place an **E** next to the ending.
2. Underline Maya's opinion statement.
3. Number the reasons Maya gives for her opinion (1, 2, 3).
4. Circle linking words that connect Maya's reasons.
5. Put a box around Maya's concluding statement.
6. Correct any errors in capitalization, punctuation, spelling, and grammar.

Try It On Your Own

Now it's your turn to take a practice writing test. Follow the steps in order. If your teacher gives you a time limit, make a plan by filling in the amount of minutes you have to complete each step.

Step 1—Choose the prompt you want to write about. Underline any key words.
(_____ minutes)

Step 2—Brainstorm for some ideas on another piece of paper. (_____ minutes)

Step 3—Fill in the organizer with your ideas. (_____ minutes)

Prompt ────────────────────────

What is your bedtime? Is it 8:30? 9:00? 9:30? If you're like most kids, you probably wish it were later. Write a paper persuading your parents to allow you to change your bedtime to a later time.

Prompt ────────────────────────

Some districts have school year-round. The students in these districts don't get a three-month summer break. Instead they get several shorter breaks throughout the year. Other districts hold school for nine months and give students the summer off. Which schedule would you prefer? Write a persuasive paper that will convince readers to agree that a year-round schedule or a nine-month schedule is best.

Topic: _____
Opinion Statement: _____
Reasons
1. _____
2. _____
3. _____

Step 4—Using your organizer as a guide, write your paper on a separate piece of paper. (_____ minutes)

Step 5—Go back and proofread your paper for mistakes in capitalization, punctuation, spelling, and grammar. (_____ minutes)

How Did You Do?

Directions: Now evaluate your own writing (or ask a friend). Complete the following steps.

Consider This

1. **Ideas/Content** Underline the opinion statement.
   - Write a number next to each reason that supports the opinion. (1, 2, 3, etc.) Put a box by the strongest reason.
2. **Organization** Is the story well structured? (yes or no)
   - Place a **B** in the margin next to the beginning, or introduction.
   - Place an **M** in the margin next to the middle.
   - Place an **E** in the margin next to the ending.
3. **Voice** Put a star by places where your personality shines through the writing.
4. **Word Choice** Circle any words that appeal to the reader's emotions.
5. **Sentence Fluency** Put a box around a section of the writing where both long and short sentences fit together smoothly. Write FLOW next to any sentences that seem too choppy.
6. **Conventions** Put a check mark above any errors in spelling, capitalization, or punctuation.

Use your answers from the **Consider This** chart to help you fill in this rubric.

Rubric — Score: *1* is the lowest; *5* is the highest					
Ideas/Content—focuses on one main idea; the details add to the main idea	①	②	③	④	⑤
Organization—has a clear beginning, middle, and end; the order is easy to follow	①	②	③	④	⑤
Voice—communicates feelings and personality; the writing is unique	①	②	③	④	⑤
Word Choice—uses colorful, fresh words in the right places	①	②	③	④	⑤
Sentence Fluency—uses both long and short sentences that flow smoothly	①	②	③	④	⑤
Conventions—few or no spelling, capitalization, and punctuation errors	①	②	③	④	⑤

I can improve my writing by _____

_____